Born in a NE industrial town, evacuated during WW11, Mavis went to Grammar school and became a teacher. She married an officer who served in both the Army and RAF and is now a widow. Her three daughters live in USA, the Lake District and Suffolk.

Mavis has travelled extensively and has written travelogues for local newspapers and magazines. She likes meeting new people, reading and dancing. Eight multitalented grandchildren keep her young and she likes to track their busy lives. After living in over 20 homes, Mavis is now settled in Ipswich.

THE MAN BEHIND

To all my wonderful family for their encouragement and support, without which I would not have had the certainty to complete this work.

Also to the stained glass window which never was.

Mavis Bensley

THE MAN BEHIND

Vanguard Press

VANGUARD PAPERBACK

© Copyright 2012
Mavis Bensley

A CIP catalogue record for this title is
available from the British Library.

ISBN 978 1 84386 839 2

Vanguard Press is an imprint of
Pegasus Elliot MacKenzie Publishers Ltd.
www.pegasuspublishers.com

First Published in 2012

Vanguard Press
Sheraton House Castle Park
Cambridge England

Printed & Bound in Great Britain

DISCLAIMER

This is a work of fiction based on biblical characters and events. It is in no way intended to be presented as true, only what might possibly have been.

Prologue

"Why are they doing this to me?"

The man stood rooted to the ground, frozen in time and space. He could hear their angry shouts, smell their foul breath and see their warped, contorted faces red with fury. He felt the venomous spittle on his skin and the pain as they jostled him, threatened with their fists and shook him. Why had they turned on him?

Only a short while ago they had been his friends and neighbours, swapping stories about the strange times they lived in.

The synagogue was always full on the Sabbath. Today, there was a buzz of excitement; so much was happening these days. Stories of a wild man eating only locusts and honey, dressed in rough clothes living in the shelter of a carob tree and preaching that the Kingdom of God is at hand. His message was urgent and powerful. 'Repent of your sins, wash them away in the River Jordan, be born again, be pure, time is short.' Some had actually heard him and been baptized. 'Could he be Moses, or Elijah sent to warn us?' they mused. 'Is he the one who will bring back the kingdom of Israel and rid us of the accursed Romans? He says he isn't and that another will come soon.' After much grumbling of taxes, atrocities and the hardships of life in general, they settled down to listening to the young teacher, one of their own villagers to read the chosen scripture.

"From the scroll of Isaiah-

'The Lord's spirit is on me because he has anointed me to preach the Good News to the poor, to tell prisoners they will be free, the blind they will see and to announce the year of God's favour has come'."

He gave the scroll back to the priest and took his seat. There was a silence as everyone watched him and waited expectantly for his comments on the reading. They were stunned by his short explanation of the Prophet's words.

"The Word has been fulfilled in your presence," he announced, gazing neither left nor right. "I am the One chosen to bring the Kingdom of God to this land."

After an even more prolonged silence, a ripple of annoyance spread through the gathered crowd.

"What did he just say?"

"Is he saying what I think he's saying?"

"Isn't he the carpenter's son?"

"This is going to cause trouble with the temple priests setting free prisoners, making the blind see. Does he mean literally perform miracles?"

"Who does he think he is, little upstart!"

"He was the snot nosed kid who chased my hens, they didn't lay for a week. I tanned his backside."

"Yes, and he broke open the cages of my doves, setting them free. I was taking them to the temple to sell for sacrifice. Lost me a load of shekels that did and when I yelled at him the little mongrel just laughed and yelled back, 'Birds are meant to fly!' then he thought he was very clever by moulding pigeons out of clay and putting them in the cages instead, cheeky brat!

What does he expect us to do? Bow down to him? No way. Not me. Blasphemer that's what he is; he ought to be run out of town." They gathered around the teacher and began to press him for more explanation, growing more abusive as he would not retract his statement that he was chosen One of God.

Two men, brothers, stood by the door of the synagogue, worried frowns on their faces and rocking uneasily. The elder gave a jerk of his head and they both walked out into the sunshine.

"This is going to get nasty," He muttered fearfully. They quickened their pace and were almost breathless when they reached home. Their mother was sitting in the garden under the shade of a fig tree. She looked up and smiled though her tranquil expression changed to anxiety when she saw the fear in their eyes.

"What has he done now?" she demanded as she hurried to join them.

"Only saying he is the chosen One of God, come to fulfil the prophecies. We've got to get him out of there, or they'll kill him." She hurried to join them as they shook their heads and gestured that she follow back to the synagogue, the angry voices of the villagers preceding them.

As they approached, the crowd was spilling out of the synagogue, pushing, shoving, shouting at her eldest son, grabbing his clothes and throwing him to the ground. His arms were bruised as he raised them to his face for protection, spittle ran down his chest and blood oozed from his nostrils. The brothers roughly charged through the crowd, shouldering them out of the way shouting, "Leave him alone, he's our brother, we'll deal with him." They in turn were shoved aside.

"Not this time. He's gone too far. He has committed blasphemy and the punishment is stoning." The inflamed crowd took up the chant. "Stone him, stone him, STONE HIM!" And like a seething entity they weaved their way up the steep hillside outside the village, their numbers swelling as women and children came out of their homes and joined the spectacle of their men folk pushing, pulling, and kicking their neighbour's son, their faces reddened with anger and malicious intent.

As they progressed the dust rose from the dirt road, kicked up into the air, rising and swirling like a cloud. His mother ran sobbing from one to another begging and beseeching them to release her son, but without prevail.

When they reached the top of the hill, the crowd quietened, partly because they were breathless from the climb, and partly because now they were wondering who would cast the first stone or who would be the one to give the final blow which would send him hurtling over the edge of the cliff to be dashed on the rocks below. They began to look at each other a little sheepishly. The brothers seized the opportunity to rush forward, raise him to his feet, and stand beside him, ready to fight off anyone who approached.

Bloodied and bruised, he raised his arms to the sky, the palms of his hands facing the now hushed mob. In a clear authoritative voice, he said slowly and deliberately,

"It is true; no prophet is ever accepted by the people of his own town. I will leave this place, shake off its dust from my feet, and never return."

He walked back down the hill again, looking neither left nor right, and speaking to no one. A pathway cleared in front of him, children clinging to their mother's skirts, men casting their eyes down, his mother being comforted by his brothers. They watched as he walked through the now settling cloud of dust, appearing to float inches above the ground,

Upon reaching the village, he walked past the synagogue, passing his boyhood home, not stopping to collect any possessions but strode onward until he had cleared the village and disappeared from view. His mother still wept at the loss of her son, and made her way home. The villagers dispersed, muttering to themselves.

'Good riddance,' seemed to be the majority verdict.

A very few wondered 'Could it be true?' But they kept their thoughts to themselves.

THE WILDERNESS

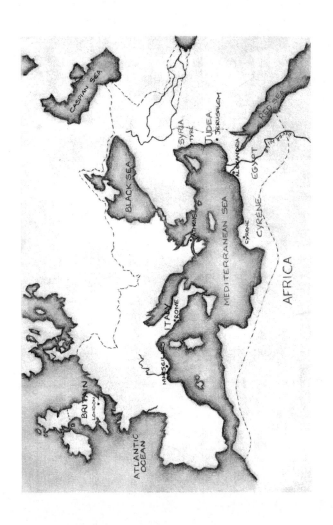

The Roman Empire

CHAPTER ONE

Solitude

The wilderness is a fearsome place. First the heat scorches the skin and sears the lungs making one almost gasp for breath. The relentless sun by day intensifies the cerulean sky and the harshness of the terrain making it shimmer in a haze of light. Few animals choose this as a place of refuge. Lizards scurry to the safety of rocks so they are not baked by the sun. Snakes, coiled to conserve body moisture, lie in shallow holes in the ground waiting and wondering when their next meal will come. Rats, foxes and wild scavenging dogs bide their time until the day's heat has gone and they can attempt to hunt their prey. Vultures, carrion crows and eagles soar on the thermals, eyes scouring the landscape, aware of the slightest movement, looking for a catch to stave off their hunger or to feed their young.

Few trees grow here, there is little or no nutrient in the baked earth to sustain anything but a few scrubby thorn bushes with spikes sharp enough to pierce the skin of an unwary animal, only beetles, lizards and scorpions survive this inhospitable terrain. Hardly any rain falls here and what moisture there is quickly dries up in the sun or soaks into the porous rock. Any morning dew rapidly cakes the sandy surface into a hardened crust.

The terrain is awesome. Far below, the green valley sinks to what must be the lowest point on earth. River water dries up leaving salt-water marshes where nothing will grow other than a few reeds or hardy grasses. The valley sides rise steeply, sometimes with sheer drops of a thousand feet. Sharp screes threaten to tear the flesh from the limbs should a wanderer miss his footing. Few men ever came here except perhaps to meditate or as fugitives, hiding from the Roman soldiers. Even bandits, zealots and thieves prefer the caves further south in the hills near the salt-water sea, protected by the mountains at Qumran. The higher landscape is pockmarked and riddled with caves, some so deep and inter-connected it is possible to get lost in the passages of darkness. The wind swirls the sand and buffets the rocks. Occasionally, sandstorms cloud the sky for days on end, the shifting sands obscuring any trail there might have been. Not even goats would venture up here willingly.

At night everything changes. Once the sun has set the burning rocks rapidly cool and at this altitude the temperature drops dramatically. Sand, aided by the wind, stings the skin and the cold bites into the limbs. Rocks, heated by day cooled by night, creak and fragment, often tumble down the mountain side like a waterfall, rumbling and crashing until they come to rest further down the slopes. Summer by day, winter by night. Not a place for ease and comfort but perfect for anyone seeking solitude and silence away from the daily grind, the materialistic world, family pressure; perfect for focusing on emotions, feelings, and thoughts of the future.

It was to this place that the man, rejected by his neighbours, friends and family came to lick his wounds and wonder where it had all gone so wrong. He scarcely noticed the hunger in his belly or his thirst although he felt the cracking of his lips as he wiped away the sand with his tongue and rolled a pebble round his mouth. His bruises had faded, only his ego still hurt.

He leaned against the boulder at the mouth of the cave which had become his place of asylum for these last few weeks. He could not remember how long he had been here Feeling the last rays of the setting sun on his face, his eyes closed, bushy eyebrows knotted together in concentration, his chin resting on his chest so that the wisps of his straggly beard gently rose and fell with his breathing, hands resting in his lap he appeared to be asleep or in deep thought. In his mind he recounted the events of the last few months.

He remembered walking for days to find his cousin who was washing away sins by totally immersing the body in the waters of the River Jordan, claiming that only pure water could cleanse the soul of past evils and make the body born again, ready to accept the Kingdom of God which, he claimed, was soon to come. As he joined the crowd, he caught sight of the wild looking man, standing up to his waist in the river, wearing a shift made from rough woven camel hair hitched up with a leather belt.

The Baptist was ranting about sinners and adulterers, more than hinting that the marriage of King Herod Antipas to his brother's wife, Herodias, whilst her first husband was still alive, was both sinful and adulterous as was his roving eye resting on Salome, his stepdaughter. Furthermore he railed against the 'vipers in the synagogue' who kowtowed to the Roman oppressors.

Eventually, when he and the Baptist were face to face, they stared at each other for quite some time as it had been many years since last they met. The wild man asked why he had come, as he recognized the one sent by God who would in future baptize with the fire of the Holy Spirit. The Baptist was persuaded by the man to immerse him in the river so this would not only wash away his sins but rightfully fulfil the prophecies. It was after the baptism that he was filled with zeal and fiery energy; he just couldn't wait to get back to his home town to proclaim the Good News to the receptive congregation in his synagogue. How wrong he had been!

He spent restless, troubled nights within the security of the cave, disturbed by the snuffling of nearby animals or squealing noises as they pounced on whatever prey they could find but more disquieted by his own thoughts. He had failed at the first hurdle in his mission to prepare the people of Israel for the coming of God's Kingdom, and was now skulking and hiding, afraid to return to his home, unsure what to do next and how to proceed. He prayed to God for guidance.

Several weeks into his solitude his peaceful existence was interrupted by the sound of someone or something scrambling up the hillside nearby. He pulled his shabby cloak around him and sank deep in the cave, not wanting to be discovered and hoped whoever it was would pass by and continue up the hillside, perhaps on some sort of hunting expedition. He could hear the sound of panting quite clearly and was startled to hear a woman's voice call out

"Yeshi, Yeshi, where are you? I know you're around here somewhere. Come out. I am not leaving till I've talked to you".

'Yeshi?' Nobody had called him by that name for years – not since his childhood days in Egypt. Memories flooded his mind with the mischievous face of a bright eyed little girl, with dark red curly hair throwing stones at a crocodile, cracking and crunching its way through the bloated body of a dead sheep which had floated down the muddy waters of the River Nile. He craned his head and peered towards the cave entrance. Silhouetted with her face still in shadow, he saw the rays of the sun catching her hair. Still curly, still auburn, and knew it was his childhood friend.

"Maryam, is it really you? How did you know where I was? What are you doing here?"

"So many questions, Yeshi! Come on out. I have brought you some water, bread and some dates. You might survive without food but you need to drink. My father and I called in at your home on our way back from Jerusalem and your mother told us what had happened. She is pretty upset you know, what were you thinking? But then, that is just like you isn't it? Act first, think later."

Still in a state of shock, he emerged from the cave and sank to the ground, greedily gulping the sweet, cool water from one of the leather pouches she had carried. Maryam settled on the rock opposite, and studied him. Not a big man, a little on the skinny side, grubby clothes, well-worn sandals, a cloak thin and faded. His hands were large with long fingers, and nails bitten down almost to the quick. It was his face she studied most whilst he drank and ate some dates wolfishly having realized just how hungry he was.

His skin was dark and toughened by the sun. High cheek bones, wide forehead almost hidden by his long hair, looking unkempt as sand and sweat had caked into it. Similarly untrimmed, his beard, wispy and uneven in length, where beads of water from the pouch had trickled and sparkled as the sun reflected on them. His eyebrows were bushy, almost touching, which gave him quite a ferocious look, but which she remembered he could waggle to make her laugh. It was his eyes that made her gasp as he shot her an appreciative glance. Deep, brown chasms that could turn almost black if he was angry, but they took on golden or amber flecks when the sun shone on his face. They were hypnotic, mesmerising and compelling, and he could hold your attention with his stare as if searching into your very soul, and reading your innermost, secret thoughts. Seconds felt like hours as Maryam gazed at him. She shivered slightly as she tore her eyes away.

"Of course I remember this place. This is where we ran away to all those years ago when you spoiled a wooden chest your father had made for a customer, remember? He cheated your father over the price saying the workmanship was poor, so you changed the carving of a cow into a pig right on the top where everyone could see it. We scuttled out of the workshop pretty quick when he came after us with a carving knife! So what are you doing? How long will you stay here? Where will you go? What next?"

"Whoa," he said, holding up his hands in mock horror, "Stop, take a breath. Now who's asking all the questions? Let's sit a while in the sunshine. I can't tell you my plans because I haven't got any. I know my goal, but not yet how to achieve it. I came up here to think and to clear my head, so for a while, let's do some catching up, right back to the time when we were kids in Egypt. You weren't even born when we first stayed with your family after our long journey to escape Herod's slaughter of innocent babies. What a madman he was! What an amazing country, I can remember all the sights; the pyramids, temples, the Nile flooding, strange people and even more strange religion. You used to follow me round like a puppy."

"Yes," she retorted, "and you used to threaten to turn me into one! We had fun in those days and I was sorry to leave but once your father said that Herod was dead and it was safe to return to Israel, my father decided to come back to our homeland. He made a good living in Egypt but his heart was always longing to take up his grandfather's fishing business in Migdahl. So that's what we did. Quite a large caravan made the journey back to the homeland, didn't it? Families dropped off at different places; Bethlehem, Jerusalem, you to Nazareth and us at our village on the Sea of Galilee.

We're doing very well now. Migdahl means 'towers'. It's where we hang the fish to dry, preserved by salt. They are delicious and we have a good business. In fact, we were just on our way back from Herod Antipas' palace delivering a huge order. My best friend Joanna is his head steward's wife, you should meet her sometime. I'm sure you would like her."

They were both silent for a while remembering their idyllic childhood. How things had changed. The oppression of the occupying Romans, then taxes that they had imposed and the extras the tax collectors added on as their cut; the clashes with local hot heads calling themselves zealots, or freedom fighters, ending in bloodshed, crucifixion, or being taken as galley slaves; the power of the high priests, appointed by the Romans, who didn't want to upset their masters and even copied Roman lifestyle in their homes. It was their job to keep the peace and the populace under control and they were content to do so.

It was a little better here in Galilee than in Judea, where the Romans had their military base and where the governor lived. Galileans didn't often go south to Jerusalem except on special occasions such as Passover week. It was many days trek and between the two states was Samaria, which although it claimed it had a Jewish population, differed greatly in its religious interpretation and there was no love lost between the people. In fact, travellers often chose to go the long way round across the other side of the River Jordan to avoid hostilities.

Galileans were regarded as country bumpkins, rough and ready, farmers, fisherman, and artisans. They did not seek conflict with their Roman masters, nor were they quite so ready to bend the knee.

Finally, they broke from their reverie. Maryam stood up and stretched her body. "I must be getting back." She said. "It's a few hours walk, and my father wants to return home. I will stay a while longer with your family and bring you some more water and maybe a little fish in a few days' time. You'll love it. What will you do?"

He thought for a moment and replied softly, "Thank you for coming, Maryam, and bringing me food and water, you have calmed me. I feel more like my old self, less agitated. I have a lot of thinking and planning to do. There must be a way to carry out God's mission for me and I will find it through prayers and meditation. Take care, little sister. Tell your father I wish him well and look forward to meeting him again soon."

He stood and watched her descending the treacherous path down the hill side, clutching at boulders and rocks to steady herself, tugging her blue cloak tightly round her. "She is still following me." He mused. "Maybe I should have turned her into a puppy after all."

CHAPTER TWO

Temptations

Left alone with his thoughts, the man spread his cloak near the entrance of the cave. He felt content, relaxed and at peace with himself. He glanced round and marvelled at the beauty of creation in this desolate place, perfect for his need for solitude. He settled on his cloak and rested his back against the side of the cave entrance. With a deep sigh he closed his eyes and began to pray for help and guidance for what he must do. After what seemed only minutes he stirred and saw that the moon had risen, casting dark shadows. A chill wind ruffled his hair but he did not seem to notice. He had professed his faith in and his love for his holy Father, had posed the questions but as yet had not received an answer. Maybe the solution had to come from within himself.

He knew all the Prophesies, had learned about Abraham, Elijah, Moses and many other ancients whose words were written in the Talmud. He knew all that was humanly possible – more, because he had interpreted their sayings in the light of who he was. He remembered the day he had run home in tears because the village bully-boys had set about him, taunting him, circling him menacingly. They did not like him because he was cleverer than they were, read more, remembered everything, was skilled at carpentry and helped his mother to look after his younger brothers and sisters. He had tried staring them out and one or two had fallen back in fear, but one of the others shouted out that his "evil eyes" did not scare them. When he made a break from the gang, one shoved him and mocked him in a sing-song voice,

"That's right, run home to your precious mummy. We're not all illegitimate you know."

Stung with humiliation, he demanded that his mother tell him what they had meant. His mother hugged him as he struggled against her until gradually his sobs came to a juddering halt. She led him outside with a cup of cool, fresh lemon juice, sweetened with wild honey and sat him on a wooden bench in the shade of a fig tree.

Slowly, keeping her emotions in check, she told him the extraordinary story surrounding his birth. When she was a very young girl, having just reached the age of puberty, she had been formally betrothed to Joseph and was soon to be married. In a vision or a dream – it was so long ago now that she was not sure which – an angel had spoken to her saying that God was pleased with her goodness and had chosen her to be the earthly mother of his holy child. She was terrified, but bravely told Joseph who was shocked and angry. Who could have defiled his beautiful Mary? She had told him she had been with no man and that it was God's child. Unbelieving, Joseph had seriously considered turning her out but then he would have been pitied or thought a fool for taking up with her in the first place. What would happen to Mary if he did? At best she would become an outcast, possibly forced into prostitution, at worst she could be stoned as an adulteress.

Joseph decided to sleep before making any decision. He too had a dream, where an angel had appeared telling him not to be afraid, that Mary's baby was indeed the child of God and would be called Emmanuel meaning *God With Us*. On waking Joseph remembered Mary's relative Elizabeth, well past child-bearing years was also having a baby and her disbelieving husband, the priest Zecheriah had been struck dumb for doubting her, so maybe anything was possible. They told friends and neighbours in Nazareth that they were going to visit Elizabeth in Judea and then Joseph had some business in Jerusalem so they would be away quite some time.

When the time came for the birth, they had travelled to Bethlehem. They had married so the child would be the legal son of Joseph who was himself descended from the royal line of King David. They had stayed at a small inn on the outskirts of Bethlehem where no one knew them. Joseph did not want one of the upper, more public rooms preferring a small room off the courtyard which was clean and airy. Travellers tied up their donkeys outside, alongside Joseph's own but no one disturbed them. Afterwards, when the baby was sleeping, three men came. They had left their sheep grazing in the fields because they had been told the Good News of the birth of a saviour in David's city, and had come to see for themselves. The new family had stayed a week in this their first home together. Their son had been circumcised according to custom and the mother had been purified.

There were other visitors to the child, strange men who had met on their journeys from far off lands. Each was a wise man, or Magus, who studied the stars and was convinced a new king had been born to rule over the Jews. They had even gone to the present King Herod and asked if he knew anything of this new king of Israel. Herod was secretly shocked and begged the Magi to return to tell him the whereabouts of the new king so that he, Herod, could come and pay homage to the newly born.

As soon as they told their story, Joseph was very disturbed. Herod was obviously up to no good and he begged the Magi not to go back to the court. They brought strange gifts, gold for a king, frankincense to burn for the spirit, and myrrh for the body. They returned to their own lands by a different route, not revealing to Herod what they had found. He was furious and ordered his soldiers to kill all the boy babies under the age of two in Bethlehem and the area round it. Joseph's anxiety had proved to be correct; he dreamed this would happen. Instead of turning north to Galilee, he travelled with Mary and the baby south to Egypt, where there was a large number of Jewish families living, and stayed there for five or six years until King Herod's death, when he had felt safe enough to come back to his old home in Nazareth.

The boy listened to this story, confused and miserable, but at the same time he felt very special. He now realized why his mother had been schooling him in the scriptures non-stop, testing him making him repeat psalms, asking him to explain what he thought the prophets meant and always making him say this prayers. He then hugged her and said everything was all right, but he needed some time to think by himself.

All this, the solitary man remembered and became even more determined to find a way to fulfil the Prophesies and prepare for the coming of God's Kingdom, which he felt very sure was imminent. He had spent many years preparing himself travelling learning, soaking up knowledge and skills. Now it was time to act; to come up with a plan. He would not, could not fail.

He thought about what kind of kingdom it would be. Maybe if he entered the priesthood, he could rise to the top, re-interpret the books of the Bible, inspire people to turn back to God and become a leader in the Sanhedrin. No, this was not the way. Too many obstacles, he would never be chosen as the High Priest by the Roman Governor, nor would he want to be. This would mean keeping the status quo and would never achieve his objectives. Perhaps he could join the Zealots, unite them into God's army of fighting men who would willingly give up their lives to free the people from the yoke of the Caesars, and take the Kingdom of Israel by force. But fighting meant killing, about which he knew nothing, and knew that this would bring down the wrath and might of Rome, leaving Israel in an even more sorry state. There had been uprisings before and the perpetrators had been hounded back into the hills and caves. The Romans had blockaded them and tried to starve them out until they chose to fling themselves to their deaths from cliff tops rather than surrender. He had no knowledge of the strategy of warfare and was unwilling to waste a single drop of blood in God's name. His Father was a god of love not wrath, of forgiveness, not punishment. So this option was rejected.

Maybe he could find a way to feed the poor and the starving as Moses had done. Make crops grow where none had grown before, and increase their harvests – that would certainly impress people! But this was not enough. To feed the body was one thing, but it was the soul and spirit which needed to be nourished. Man cannot live by bread alone, people's hearts must be full not just their bellies.

Perhaps it needs to be something spectacular, he thought, to make them believe in me. I could go to the Temple in Jerusalem on the Sabbath day where many people would be gathered. I could tell them that I am the Son of God in human form, and just as any father would do anything to prevent harm coming to his children, so my father would protect me. I could then climb to the highest point of the temple and fling myself off, safe in the knowledge that not a single hair of my head would be damaged or my foot dashed against a stone. Surely that would be enough to prove what I say is the truth. The people, the priests, even the Romans could not then deny they had witnessed a miracle, and that the son of the one true God was living here on Earth.

He mulled over these options in his mind for many days, trying to decide which path to take. Suddenly he sat up straight, his eyes wide as he realized all these tempting solutions were wrong. Earthly glory or power was not for him, God was not part of a circus to be gawped at or put to the test. Where had these stupid ideas come from? Not from God, certainly. They were not only stupid, but wicked, and could only have come from the Fallen Angel. He stood, pulled himself up and shouted

"Get thee behind me Satan! Do not test me in this way. I worship the Lord my God and serve him only."

The first rays of the light of a new day gave the sky a rosy glow. The air was full of promise. Exhausted by his efforts to find a solution, the man wrapped his cloak round his shoulders and slept.

CHAPTER THREE

The Pupil

After a long, deep, dreamless sleep, he woke refreshed, light-hearted, ready to face the day and a new chapter in his life. Having resisted the temptations to create the Kingdom of God on an earthly, materialistic basis, he knew without a shadow of a doubt, that a plan would formulate in his mind and would be one that he was able to carry out, no matter what the consequences were.

He decided to go about his planning logically, knowing he would have to make a big impact on as many people as possible in a very short time because the day of reckoning would soon be here, maybe even in his own lifetime. He had long since stopped asking himself, "Why me?" And accepted that he was the Chosen One with great responsibilities – more than all the other prophets put together, everything which had been foretold was leading up to this moment in the history of the Jews. Was he up to the task? He needed faith in both God and himself. He had never doubted the love of his Father and was determined to live up to His expectations. He needed courage to stand up to verbal and physical abuse which was sure to come. This did not concern him too much, as he could match any critic or adversary with God's help. He also needed knowledge and understanding.

It seemed that all his life he had been learning, soaking up knowledge like sand absorbing water. His mother was his first teacher, telling him Bible stories, teaching him how to read the scriptures and to explain them for himself. When her knowledge was exhausted, she encouraged him to study further under the tutelage of an old and distant relative called Hillel, who was a labourer by day and a preacher in the synagogue and temple at other times. Hillel marvelled at the boy's understanding of almost every subject and often they discussed issues and problems of the day as equals, rather than pupil and master. They spoke of the law, the commandments, present-day religious leaders, and the role of the Pharisees, especially under Roman rule. They spoke of the Sadducees who were often rich traders travelling the known world and bringing foreign influences back to Judea as well as cargos of spices, precious metals, cloth and jewels.

Then they would discuss the plight of the poor. These people made up the majority of the population. Most of them were hard-working individuals who just wanted a decent life for their families, to live in peace and to worship God in their own way. They kept the Laws, observed the Sabbath, paid their taxes and prayed for better days to come.

It was common knowledge that a messiah was coming and soon. There had even been men who proclaimed themselves to be the messiah, performing miracles but they had quickly been shown to be charlatans or false prophets wanting earthly adulation. Nevertheless, there was a frisson of excitement and urgency in the air, stirred up by John the Baptist, an expectation and hope for a new leader, or king to emerge following in King David's footsteps.

He now remembered one of Hillel's instructions.

"What is hateful to you, do not unto another" and how he had suggested it would be better to say, "What you wish men to do to you, do so unto them," because it was a more positive way of looking at things. He made a mental note that one of the things he wanted to do was not challenge the laws of the Jews, but change them with a more positive interpretation.

The next big influence on his acquisition of knowledge was to listen to discussions between learned men as they sat in the courtyard of the Jerusalem Temple. Here all the great teachers, priests, politicians, and doctors of the day would talk about or argue over current issues, religious and temporal. Sometimes, even though he was only a boy of thirteen, he would join in posing his opinions and comments, which for the main part were encouraged and taken seriously. Once though, he had upset them, especially the priests, by asking why they felt the need to make sacrifices. He had felt nauseous from the acrid smell of burning meat, feathers and wool. He protested saying,

"Does it really please God to smell this smoke, and does he really want the poor to spend their money on sacrifices when they could better feed their children?" Outraged, the priests had retorted

"It is the law! Do you think you know more about the law than we do? Get along with you, and find something else to do, rather than argue with your elders and betters. Go home to your family."

It was only then that he had realized he had not seen his parents for several days, and that they might be looking for him. His mother had chastised him for staying behind, which took him by surprise, for she of all people should have known that he was about his Father's business.

Thoughts of his earthly father, Joseph, flooded his mind. He felt a little ashamed of his dealings and attitude towards him. He could have been more respectful instead of being more passive towards him. He regretted he had not been at home when Joseph had died some years earlier, and that he had not comforted his mother, other than to tell her that Joseph was in a much better place. One small incident came to mind which made him smile, however. Many years earlier, Joseph had made a beautiful carved bed frame for an important client, and at the last minute he found he had made a tiny mistake in the measurement of a side piece, which meant there was a weakness in the frame. The client was due that day to collect his furniture and Joseph was distraught that he would have to delay the sale and make a new piece. His eldest son touched his arm and winked. Amazed, Joseph watched as his son closed his eyes, stroked the offending undersized piece of wood, easing it along until it clicked into place, fitting perfectly. They both stared at it, then father and son hugged each other and laughed uproariously as the client approached the carpenter's work place. That had been a joyful moment; one of only a very few in their relationship.

His sources of learning seemed to dry up and he became restless, without direction and aimless, so his mother called on another relative for help. His name was also Joseph but he came from the area of Arimathaea. She smiled as she remembered her son had struggled saying Joseph of Arimathaea and had nicknamed him uncle Jofa which had stuck. Joseph was a rich merchant, owning many ships which plied their trade across the sea to cities such as Ephesus and Rome itself, Greek cities, the islands of Crete and Malta, on to Gaul and further to the recently conquered island of Albion, sometimes known as Britannia. Amongst his other interests he was an expert on mining and was an adviser to the Romans on mines, metals and trade. He was a member of the Sanhedrin in Jerusalem so had a good knowledge of what was going on in the world, both locally and further afield.

It was to Joseph that Mary entrusted her eldest son, to travel and learn the ways of people outside their own land. Galilee itself was a busy trading crossroads, with caravans of traders from Egypt and Arabia journeying north to Phoenicia, Syria and Babylon, returning laden with more goods and gossip to trade. Always, occupying Roman troops travelled the length and breadth of the Roman Empire, so there was never a shortage of work for the shipping industry. Joseph had several ships anchored at Caesarea Maritima and other vessels at the port of Tyre. He had a full load almost ready to sail from Tyre so had no problem taking Mary's son on board but warned her that the lad would have to work his passage. Even though he looked stern and serious he managed to give Mary a small wink which reassured her.

And so it was that over the next couple of years the lad experienced all the trials and tribulations of seafarers. He worked as a cabin boy, fetching, carrying and cleaning for Joseph and the captain. He swabbed decks, hoisted sails, learned about ropes, knots and rigging, he hefted bales of wool, sacks of grain and amphorae of wine and water. He suffered severe storms, was soaked by waves and buffeted by strong winds. He even took turns pulling on the heavy wooden oars learning how to keep even, rhythmic strokes with the other oarsmen. One thing he did learn very quickly was that everyone on board ship was part of a team, although having different functions they all worked towards the same goal if they were to reach port safely. There was only one master however, who encouraged, cajoled, even threatened his crew whilst guiding them towards success.

When in port, he marvelled at the beautiful buildings, especially the magnificent temples where so many different gods were worshipped. There seemed to be a different one for every facet of human life, earth, sea, sky, sun, moon, crops beauty, war, music, poetry, wine and love – they were all there. Each god had a different name according to which country the ship anchored in. He was amazed that people from such advanced civilizations could not grasp that there was only one God who had created all these earthly things and that He alone should be worshipped.

Just as he grew in knowledge, languages and other skills, he also grew in stature, was taller, leaner, stronger. Muscles in his arms, legs and back strengthened until he could pull his weight with the best of the sailors. It was with regret that he eventually left the ship with its cargo of tin and ferocious hunting dogs, from that strange, cold place that he fleetingly visited called Britannia. He had met rough, resentful people called Celts who painted their bodies with blue dye but who loved the cargo of wine Jofa had taken on board in Greece.

He bade farewell to his uncle and returned somewhat reluctantly to Nazareth. His family welcomed him home wholeheartedly and listened to his stories of his travels in awe and wonderment. Maybe now he would settle down to normal family life in the village, but in her heart Mary knew that it would not be long before her son regained his wanderlust and once more left home.

CHAPTER FOUR

The Lost Years

Although the cave provided security, shelter from the biting winds or blazing sun, a place of peace where he could meditate and pray, the man preferred to walk in the surrounding countryside, scrambling up the mountains running down the screes as his mood changed. Many thoughts, ideas and plans passed through his mind as to how he should proceed with his mission. Frustration and elation went hand in hand as he discarded some aspects as unworkable or inappropriate or when his mind cleared and the way forward became feasible and even obvious. He knew the expectations of the Israelites and pondered how to get his message across. But what was his message?

All his thoughts had to be clarified and made logical. He must be well prepared, as there would be opposition from many quarters. He knew he couldn't blunder again as he had done in his own synagogue. He had to be subtle, not break any law, only bend it a little, amend it somewhat so that negative aspects became positive. Sometimes at night he would lie under the stars, his cloak wrapped tightly round him and look up to the heavens and beyond into the inky emptiness, totally absorbed in his thoughts, prayers and at oneness with his Father, his God, his creator and with the universe, finally at peace with himself and secure in the knowledge that his time had come to convince and prepare the people for the coming of God's Kingdom on earth. Although he had learned many skills in the past, he accepted that he was only human, only one man needing the guiding hand of his Father and help from his fellow men to achieve his aim. Time was short and he must act quickly to create an impact.

Inevitably, tiny doubts crept into his mind, the 'what if?' thoughts as he pondered various scenarios. He needed to test his plans and fine tune them but how and with whom?

There were fences to be mended with his family but he felt he could not confide in them as his brothers especially were sceptical, and his mother, although she knew he had a great task to perform, was not sufficiently worldly wise to advise him or comment on his strategies. Uncle Jofa would be ideal to see the strengths and flaws of his plans but he was many days sailing away and therefore could offer no help so who could he turn to?

A sudden beam of evening sunlight hit upon a small bush outside the cave, highlighting the leaves that fluttered in the breeze. They seemed to turn into a dark red colour almost like auburn curls.

"Of course," he muttered to himself. "Who was it that sought me out in this place, brought me food and drink? Maryam! I have not seen her for many years and yet I felt thoroughly at home with her. She who made me laugh and relax, with whom I felt empathy, a friend, an equal, one who filled the void inside me. She is the one I can tell anything to, one who I can trust. She is intelligent, clear thinking, worldly wise and knowledgeable. She is the one who will help me to hone my thoughts and ideas. Why didn't I think of her straight away! I feel she knows me well and has been loyal since childhood. She will make an ideal sounding board!"

Concentrating on the bush which by now had turned an even darker red as the sun sank lower, he placed his hands in his lap, his fingers lightly touching he breathed deeply and slowly. He emptied his mind of all thoughts, internally uttering his mantra which he had learned many years ago as a method of concentration until a darkness filled his vision and his eyes closed. Out of the darkness came a pinprick of light which widened and brightened until he could see a picture of his mother's house. He could see Mary preparing an evening meal, his sisters, Salome and Mary chatting together on stools in the corner of the room. His brother James, always so devout, was praying near a wall. His knees had developed callouses from so much kneeling that he had earned the nickname 'Camel Knees'.

Maryam entered the room carrying platters of food for the table. He watched as she joined in the general chatter seeming to fit in so well into the family scene. He intensified his thoughts on her, willing her to think of him. He told her he needed to see her and soon. Over and over he silently called her name intermingled with "Yeshi," He saw her shudder and cast a glance over her shoulder to the doorway as if expecting to see him walk through it. She pressed her hands to her head as though to quell a headache, left the room and stepped outside into the cool evening air, looking round fearfully.

"I know you're here somewhere Yeshi," she whispered "or is it just my demons returning to punish me for thinking about you so much? I can't get you out of my mind. I was determined not to see you again as you seem to have no room for a woman in your life, but I can't resist coming just one more time, if only to try to heal the rift in your family."

She looked up to the darkening sky, now streaked with rosy clouds and saw the first evening star. A slight breeze brushed her face, light as a kiss making her shiver as her fingers touched her lips and she returned the kiss in the direction of the wilderness.

"Tomorrow, Yeshi," she promised.

Before sunrise the next morning the man strode out to find a prominent mound from which he could see far down the hillside, anticipating the way Maryam would come. He had awakened early, prayed his thanks to God for giving him inspiration and eagerly awaited her arrival. As he watched the dusty road below, he saw Roman horsemen travelling south, overtaking merchant caravans laden with goods to trade maybe as far away as Egypt or north to Phoenicia and beyond.

His heart was saddened as he saw a lone traveller set upon by bandits, clubbed, robbed and left for dead at the side of the road. It was unusual for a sole traveller to be on the road which lead south through Samaria. Most Jews preferred to travel the long way round to Judea by crossing the Jordan River as the Samaritans, although professing the Jewish faith were at variance with traditional Jewish beliefs. They were often aggressive towards travellers.

As he watched, too far away to be of assistance himself, a priest approached the victim but he was in a hurry to get to the synagogue and not wishing to contaminate himself by touching an unclean person, he slapped his donkey and went on his way on the other side of the road. Other travellers, presuming the man dead and having witnessed this type of scene many times before, hurried on lest they too should be accosted by the same band of robbers. Eventually a man, who from the look of his girth probably weighed more than his donkey, stopped and eased himself down by the fallen victim. He could tell from the way the big man was dressed that he was a Samaritan. Would he finish the job and kill the injured man?

Instead, and not without effort, the Samaritan managed to lift the body and place him across the donkey, having first given him a few drops of water from his leather water-carrier and wiped the blood from his face and hair. He then proceeded on his way leading his donkey and not troubled by having to walk several miles to the next village in the rising heat on feet not used to walking more than a few steps at a time.

Much impressed the watcher learned another lesson about man's love for fellow man even if he was a supposed enemy. To love and care was a human trait which surmounted all laws and boundaries. This message of love and humanness was very important to get across in his mission.

So deep in thought was he, that he did not hear Maryam's approach and was startled by her calling his name. He looked up and saw her smiling face framed by that gorgeous mop of curly hair. Impulsively he rushed up to her pulled her off the donkey she was riding hugged her tightly and lifting her off the ground, twirled her round and round. So shocked was she at the actions of this skinny, unshaven, smelly madman that her body became rigid and she pounded him with her fists.

"Put me down at once!" she yelled. "Have you been affected by the sun that you are behaving so strangely?" Without letting go, he stood her on a low rock, eyes smiling, the words tumbling out of his mouth. Without seeming to take a breath, he told her of his plans for his life's work; to teach all people, gentiles included, about the loving God and how to accept His kingdom in their hearts. How he needed a team to work together like they did on Jofa's ships. He needed to show people that he was different from all the other prophets. He wanted impact on large numbers of people and quickly. That he would meet opposition from the Romans and more than likely from priests of his own faith as well as the politicians who were content with their own way of life, was inevitable.

He would probably suffer humiliation, pain, degradation and maybe even death if it is the will of his Father.

As he babbled away unceasingly about his plans his grip on Maryam relaxed and she was able to tear herself away. Most of his ramblings had been totally incomprehensible to her and she feared his religious fervour had turned his mind.

"Stop!" she commanded. "Take hold of yourself. Slow down, take a breath. I don't know what you are talking about. If you don't stop behaving so wildly I will leave immediately and tell your family there is no hope for you, ever. I've got a message for you from your mother, by the way, but let's get out of the sun first, calm down, eat and drink. Then we will talk properly. I'm hungry, tired and dusty from the journey here and my mind is in a whirl from all the ranting I have just had to endure!"

Stunned at being so abruptly interrupted from his outpourings, he looked anxiously at her face and saw fear in her eyes. He realized he had repeated his mistake at the synagogue once again by rushing out words before thinking them through! The last thing he wanted to do was scare her off. She of all people had to believe, help and support him. He smiled his acquiescence, mumbled "I'm sorry. I didn't mean to frighten you." He held out his hand which she took and gently lead both her and the donkey back to the calming coolness of his temporary home in the cave.

Before eating he dampened a cloth and wiped much of the grime from his face and hands, ran his fingers through his tousled hair and unkempt beard in an attempt to restore himself to a semblance of normality. He kept apologizing for frightening her saying he only wanted her to share his excitement.

She picked at some bread whilst remembering the thrill of his arms around her but managed to look at him sternly whilst wondering if his embrace had been solely due to his excitement or whether he felt more than just brotherly love towards her. Putting these thoughts to one side she opened the conversation by telling him his mother's message.

"There is to be an important wedding in Cana in a few weeks' time. The whole family has been invited, including you. Both the bride and groom's families are old friends so there will be no animosity towards you and that you should come. It will be a fine opportunity to make up with your brothers, so what do you say? Will you come?"

"We'll see," was his only reply. "I've got so much to think about at the moment."

"I know that," she said. "You have got to get everything straight in your mind otherwise you will fail before you have even begun. Let's start by me telling you what I know about you and we will go from there." She had such a calming effect on him that he settled back against the cave wall, utterly comfortable in her presence.

"I know about your birth from your mother," she started, "and that frightened me. I understand now how you could do those weird things in Egypt when we were children. I am aware of your passion, no obsession, for learning from whom so ever, whatever and wherever you could.

Your mother told me of your travels with your uncle Joseph to strange lands. She said you also travelled for many years to different places and that when you finally returned a year or so ago you were much changed, but couldn't quite express how in words.

I also sense it, Yeshi, and it scares me so much. I am your friend but I see an aura about you. You are a man but there is something else, something intangible, a presence, something that makes me wary. I want to touch you and be normal but I am afraid." Her voice trembled with emotion and suddenly her whole body began to shake, her head lolled back and her eyes rolled in their sockets. Her hands and arms twitched and her legs jerked spasmodically. Froth foamed from her mouth and her head banged on the cave floor. He was immediately on his knees at her side, grasping her head firmly until she was facing him but unseeing.

"Maryam, I have you safe. I will never hurt you, do you believe me? You know who I am, do you believe in me?" Her eyelids fluttered and her mouth tried to form words but her tongue would not conform. Still holding her head he laid her down gently then raised his eyes and voice to heaven, entreating his Father's help to cast out the demons which had tortured Maryam's body and tormented her soul for many years. Eventually, her shaking body stilled. She murmured softly, "I hear you Yeshi, I believe in you, I love you." Then she slept peacefully for many hours,

When she woke the sun was sinking below the horizon. Hues of olive and brown were changing to purple and black. Shadows chased each other to cover the whole of the hillside. Fearing that she was alone and would have to spend the night alone in the cave and maybe attacked by wild animals, she called out for Yeshi.

He was just outside tying up the donkey for the night, making sure it had straw to eat and pouring some water for it to drink. He had already taken the supplies it had brought into the cave and had bolted down a meal of bread and the special salt fish which Maryam had promised. It was, as she had said, delicious. He too felt tired and drained but only left Maryam's side for a few minutes at a time. Sure in the knowledge that she would never again be troubled by her demons, he felt happy and contented that she had admitted believing in him, that she said she loved him was an added bonus and confirmed his choice of confidante.

It didn't bother him that the role of women in his society in general was to be subservient, to be treated sometimes worse than animals. He knew that some strong minded women, of whom Maryam was one, could hold their own, become business women, landowners, could trade, argue and become rich and powerful in their own right. She was his equal in intelligence, stamina, determination and now in faith. She would not falter even if events turned out badly for them. He knew she would be at his side, encouraging or restraining him wherever their fortunes lead. It surprised him that he was now thinking in terms of 'we' and 'us', but once again he reminded himself that he was human and that the love of another human being did not detract from his love of God his Father, maybe even enhanced it because now he was being re-enforced and reassured by a partner.

Upon hearing her voice, he rushed into the cave, sat down beside her and raised her fingertips to his lips.

"They're gone, those demons will never hurt you again." he promised. She sighed with relief when she saw him and cupped his face in her hands.

"I feel so good," she uttered. "As though a great stone has been lifted from my head. I want to dance and sing. Thank you Yeshi. How did you do it? Where did you learn such things?"

"It's a long story. I have learned many things over the years, Maryam," he replied.

"But, the one thing above all else is that I cannot do anything alone. God works through me. Without Him, I am nothing."

"This story of yours," she said. "Tell it to me. What do you hope to achieve, what did you learn, where did you go, who did you meet, what did you…" He interrupted her with a laugh and put his hand over her mouth and an arm round her shoulders.

"Now whose tongue is running away with itself? It is a long story as I have said but as it is too dark for you to return to Nazareth you might as well hear all the details of my last few years. It will pass the time until you feel the need for sleep again."

They settled down in the comparative warmth of the cave, wrapped in their cloaks and protected from the stone floor by the blanket which Maryam had used as a saddle on the donkey on her way up here. They could hear the donkey rhythmically chomping on the straw and gently snuffling as it too settled down for the night. They could hardly make out each other's shape in the darkness but were comfortably aware of each other's presence as he began his story.

"After I returned from sailing with Jofa I couldn't settle. I had learned so much from many different cultures but mainly it was what God's Kingdom should not be like. I knew my scriptures and the temple priests' teachings but it was still not enough. I needed more, so I travelled south with a group of merchants heading for Jericho.

I had heard of a group of Jewish visionaries called Essenes who had separated themselves off from other people, living on the Qumran plateau near the Dead Sea. They devoted their lives to prayer, strongly believing that the end of time and God's judgment was very near. They were great thinkers and writers with a whole library of manuscripts stored in huge stone jars. They lived a life of dedication and purity. They hated the Romans and anyone, Jews or gentiles who traded or socialized with them.

I found their ways too harsh and narrow for how I envisioned the kingdom of God, so I felt I had to move on yet again. This time I met up with some merchants who were travelling east along the Great Silk Road. One man in particular interested me. He came from a far off land called India and invited me to stay with him for a while.

The priests in his religion are called Brahmins from whom I learned much, such as the healing powers of herbs and medicines, relaxation of the mind and meditation. I could empty my mind until it seemed I did not exist. I did not even notice the heat of the day or the bitter cold of the night in the mountains.

What I did not like about their religion was their caste system and told them that God loves all men equally. They were furious at this, and I had to leave quickly into the back streets of the town where the so called 'untouchables' scraped a living as best they could. They believed they would have to live many lifetimes to be anywhere near God and were astonished when I taught them a new way of life, and that God loved them just as much as the Brahmins and if they were sincere in their prayers to him, they didn't even need priests to tell them what to do or not to do, or even intercede on their behalf with God. I am afraid the Brahmins thought I was a traitor for criticizing their beliefs, so I retreated even further into the mountains.

I was overcome by the beauty and majesty of this place. There were great, snow-capped peaks, glistening in the sun or covered by swirling mists and dense clouds. Waterfalls, thin and gossamer-like or wild and thunderous, crags split by frost and time, cutting, savage winds lashing at one's clothes and body, brilliant, almost blinding sunshine, or dark storm clouds rolling across the sky casting ominous shadows as though in waves of anger. Sheer drops of hundreds of feet threatened unwary travellers. Moss covered rocks, slippery from mist and melted snow, spelled danger at every step. Trails twisted and turned as they snaked up the valley or rock sides, sometimes wide enough for an ox cart, other places barely wide enough for a single traveller or even a mountain goat. Eagles and vultures soared on the rising winds looking for prey, afraid of nothing and no one.

The air is so thin that the lungs burn as they work extra hard, and you gasp for air to stay alive. Shallow breaths help in meditation, the heart beat slows until it almost seems to stop.

One becomes aware of the inner self to the exclusion of external conditions. Cold, heat, hunger, pain, wind, snow, day and night are as nothing.

Here is a good place to commune with God, to become one with the universe, make sense of the past, and to anticipate the future. I delved further into the meanings of the Prophesies, the evil of worshipping false gods, the love of one true God, and how he works through all living things. The flowers of the fields, beasts of burden, the sick and the poor, especially those who live simply and who open their hearts to God and their fellow man. He created the laws of nature, and if our bodies are at one with nature, we will be healthy. Illness can be rectified through nature and faith in an omnipotent God. I do not know what it is like to be sick. Never in my life have I had an illness. A healer inspires faith so I must try to heal as many sick people as I can.

In those mountains I felt so close to God, as if I could touch Him. I could see Him when I closed my eyes. I could feel His presence in the wind and smell His sweetness in the freshness of the air around me and in the scent of the earth beneath my feet. Everything was straightforward and clear to me.

If only I can get this simplicity across in my mission which is soon to come, to people whose lives have become so complicated, materialistic and integrated with the lives of our oppressors, to those who have it easy because they pay lip service to God, make sacrifices and pay their dues in the temple but have no humility in their hearts.

The stillness of that place was filled with the overwhelming power of God, His bounty, His urgency that the time is right. The end of time is near and just as my body then was scourged by the winds, shut down from the lack of air, nearly died from the cold or could have been broken by a false step on the rocky paths, so must I suffer in the time to come. I hope to bring my message of love and hope to a people who are almost broken by the yoke of occupation, apathy or self-delusion but who are waiting for the fulfilment of the prophesies of Isaiah, Elijah and Moses which I can and will deliver. I realized that God is everywhere and that we do not need to travel to find Him. He is within us and loves us more than our earthly father."

He paused for a moment to sip some water and waited for Maryam to comment but all he heard was her gentle breathing against his shoulder and he wondered how long she had been asleep and how much she had heard of his story. It didn't really matter as he had been glad to remind himself of how much he had learned over the last ten or fifteen years and how he could put it to good use. He sighed and let the darkness wash over him as he finally succumbed to peaceful sleep with Maryam's warm body resting comfortably beside him.

CHAPTER FIVE

Maryam

The first light of day streamed through the cave entrance. Tinged with an orange hue, it gave an eerie glow to the semi darkness inside. Maryam shivered, but it was not the coldness which had awakened her. There was something else, something strange which had disturbed her sleep. Cautiously she cast her eyes round the gloom but saw nothing. There it was again, a barely audible sound, like the hum of insects, a droning noise "aummmmmmmmmmmmm". Now fully awake, her wits alerted, she scrambled to the mouth of the cave to find Yeshi.

What she saw startled her. He was sitting cross legged, his face tilted to the sun. His elbows rested on his knees, hands almost in prayer, fingers scarcely touching. It was as if he was carved in stone, so still was he, and yet it was from him this deep guttural, humming sound emanated.

She approached gingerly, not wanting to break his concentration – if that's what it was, and sat nearby waiting patiently. She thought he seemed so much younger in this morning light. Lines had disappeared from his face. He looked so peaceful and yet so totally absorbed. As she watched him she also became more relaxed and seemed to drift off to sleep although her eyes were wide open. As she gazed at him, he turned to her and smiled. He held out his hand which she took. Her vision seemed to blur slightly then cleared again, but now she saw not only Yeshi, but crowds of people all smiling and waving palm branches, shouting something she could not quite make out. As she watched, the smiling faces disappeared replaced by angry expressions, and the palm branches changed to fists threatening him. Maryam dropped his hand and shrank back in horror. The crowds disappeared and all was as before; the sunny mountainside, Yeshi sitting eyes closed, cross legged and seemingly oblivious to her presence.

"Have my demons returned to torment me?" she asked herself. "Yeshi help me."

"I don't know what's happening."

Although she had not spoken out loud, he turned to her, now fully awake and said, "There are no more demons, I told you that. Now tell me what you saw." She told him of the happy smiling people round him who suddenly changed to a threatening, murderous mob. "It seemed so real Yeshi and yet there is nothing here. Was it a dream?"

"It was more than a dream, Maryam. It was a vision of what is to come. I tried to convey to you that I will be successful and that people will believe in me but then so easily they will turn against me. It will happen and there is nothing I can, or want to do to change it because it is God's will."

"You did this thing to me Yeshi? But how? You were deep in thought."

"Not in thought Maryam, in meditation or a deep trance, where you are free from distraction. Consciousness slips away and there is nothing, your mind is empty. There is no colour or shape. Only God can enter your mind."

"Tell me about this emptiness you speak of. What is it like?" she asked, eager to soak up all he could tell her.

"It is hard to explain in words," he replied, taking her hand. "Think of it as being awake and being asleep. When we are awake we can hear, smell, touch, see and taste things. Our mind interprets this information. When we sleep, perhaps we dream, the mind acts out a story that we may or may not be a part of. When we don't dream our minds are empty, there is nothing. We don't remember falling asleep, it just happens.

It is this state that I go into when I meditate. What you heard was a noise called a mantra – something I say to help me concentrate. It is 'AUM' which means 'I AM'."

Maryam looked thoughtful as she tried to absorb what he had said. "It sounds frightening to me," she commented. "Could you die in this state? It seems as though you have no control."

To which he replied, "Could you die in your sleep? Anything is possible, but what is death? The breath leaves the body and it shuts down. The soul is no longer needed and joins with the spirit to be with God. Then, there is no more pain and suffering. As for being in control, I can regulate my meditation, set a period of time or simply reduce my concentration to return to consciousness."

Maryam frowned. "Well that is good, if you need to concentrate and shut out the world," she snapped, "but from what I understand you have this mission, a prophesy to fulfil so you need to be more practical, earthly and frankly more realistic! Sitting around meditating might get you close to God, but it won't help to bring His kingdom to the masses, so we need to talk ideas and ways to succeed."

He threw back his head and gave out a deep, throaty laugh, startling the donkey which started braying. Maryam looked in amazement at the pair, then giggled and joined in the cacophony of sound until tears ran down her face. Eventually the laughter subsided and he wiped his eyes with his sleeve.

"Oh Maryam you are so good for me," he chortled. "You know exactly what to do and say. Of course you are right. I don't have long, two, maybe three, years to achieve my goal. First I need a team, a small group of people who will believe in what I am trying to do. I will teach them about healing and about God's kingdom, then they will spread the word to other people. Maybe John who baptized me would be good to start with, although he can be a bit wild and unpredictable," he said thoughtfully.

Maryam's eyes darkened, she frowned and sadness shadowed her face.

"Oh Yeshi," she whispered, lowering her head. "You cannot have heard out here. John has been executed by Herod Antipas. The news spread like wildfire, people are so angry. I'm sorry to be the one to tell you."

His eyes opened wide with shock and disbelief. "Why? How? When did it happen?" He struggled to get the words out. He was so horrified his tongue seemed to stick to the roof of his mouth.

Tears in her eyes, Maryam told him what her friend, Joanna, who was the wife of the chief steward at Herod's court, had told her when she was in Jerusalem.

"She said that Herod had promised his stepdaughter anything if she would dance for him which she did. Then she asked for John's head on a platter. Everyone was shocked of course, but Herod could not refuse her, so soldiers were sent to behead John, who was already in prison. It must have been a dreadful sight! My friend said she suspects Salome's mother was behind this disgusting request. Herodias, Herod's wife was furious with John for calling her an adulteress and this was her spiteful revenge. So, no, Yeshi you cannot have John as part of your team, but many of his followers are still living in or around Galilee. I suggest you go there to recruit your following."

His eyes flashed with anger.

"That murderous fox and I will meet one day. God will punish him for all the evil he has done, for being a weak king and for paying homage to the Romans." He took a deep breath. "I must put this behind me and go forward with more determination than ever. The time has come for positive action. I will stay in this place just a little while longer. I must be practical though, so I will need your help, Maryam. If I have a group of disciples who will follow me everywhere, they must be fed and given shelter. I have some relatives and contacts but not enough to sustain a lengthy campaign."

Maryam quickly broke in. "I have money," she gushed. "I have a good business in weaving and dyeing fine woollen cloth as well as what I can earn from selling my father's fish. Also I have many good friends who will help, I'm sure. I must return to Migdahl soon. My father will be worried about my delay, but I will see you again when you come to Capernaum. I will count the days." So saying, she leapt to her feet and untethered the donkey.

He helped to spread the blanket over the patient animal's broad back and fastened the now empty pots on one side. As she turned to hoist herself up, he caught her by the waist, pulled her to him abruptly and kissed her, long and deep. It was like a lightning bolt shooting through them leaving them both breathless. When they finally broke apart they did not speak for several minutes, silently giving each other their commitment.

Eventually, his voice a little husky, he said, "Thank you Maryam, you have helped me so much. In fact from now on I will call you 'Mara' meaning 'my teacher' and I too will count the days until we meet again."

"You will always be 'Yeshi' to me," she said softly against his cheek. "You may be a teacher, a rabbi, God's son or whatever else other people may call you but to me, you are simply 'Yeshi' – my love." She pulled away from his grasp reluctantly. "I don't want to, but I must go now."

He lifted her by the waist and gently settled her side saddle on the donkey, gave a final beaming smile then clicked his tongue to set the donkey on its way.

'By the way," he shouted at her retreating figure. "Tell her 'Yes'."

Puzzled she halted and turned to look at him.

"Yes, what?" she queried.

"Tell my mother that I will come to the wedding at Cana and that I will see her in a few days' time."

She waved in reply, kicked the donkey's side with her sandaled foot and continued down the mountainside, still savouring the tingling on her lips.

He watched until she was out of sight then returned to the cave to spend one last night, alone and in prayer in the wilderness. He sighed turned his face to the heavens and spoke out loud,

"IT HAS BEGUN!"

THE MISSION

The Holy Land at the time of Christ

CHAPTER SIX

The Prodigal Returns

He approached his home with trepidation. Would the villagers still want to stone him or keep him out of Nazareth? Would they ignore him, beat and spit on him or shout curses he wondered. He held his head high and strode purposefully down the road hiding the fear he felt in his pounding heart. His mouth was dry and his eyes darted everywhere ready for anything unusual indicating an attack. Thankfully he reached his mother's house without incident and sank gratefully onto a couch in the cool inner room.

His mother rushed towards him, dropping the dish she was carrying. If she was dismayed at his dishevelled appearance she did not show it.

"Welcome home my son!" she cried hugging him tightly. "I'm so glad to see you. You've been away too long. I was worried about you. Everyone was until Maryam came back a few days ago and told us that you were in good spirits." Giving him a sideways glance she added, "She looked as though she was in good spirits also. It's a pity she had to go back to

Migdahl so soon. I enjoyed having her round the house. She told me that you had cured her of her demons. That was a good thing to do. The poor girl has suffered enough over the years. No man would marry such a woman, regarded as mad, tainted and unclean because of those unfortunate attacks. Yet, she is one of the kindest, most intelligent, thoughtful people I know. She has always had a soft spot for you, my son. You too are well past marrying age. Maybe the two of you should settle down together and be happy."

He gave her a knowing smile and said, "One day maybe, if it is God's will but for the immediate future my plans do not include marriage. You know that I have a special mission that I must complete. The time has come, it will be hard and possibly dangerous, but I cannot delay any longer. The Zealots and Siccari have tried to restore the kingdom of Israel to the Jewish people by their rebellions, uprisings, and attacks on the Romans, but have so far failed. Mine is a different approach. It will be a groundswell amongst the ordinary people and one which I hope will cause no bloodshed. There has been too much hounding and slaughter of the rebels, too much persecution and retribution on their behalf. Everyone has seen the lines of crucifixion victims. There is a wide spread feeling of anger and abandonment. I will bring hope to the people, a belief that God's Kingdom is coming and soon. I cannot do it by sitting at home with a wife and family. In a few days I am setting out for Capernaum but first I will make my peace with my brothers, that is, after I have bathed, put on fresh clothing, and of course eaten."

Later that evening, his brothers James, Joseph, Simon, and Jude returned home, hungry from their labours in the carpenter's workshop and the fields. They were surprised to hear the sounds of laughter and chattering coming from their garden. The aroma of roasting chicken and lamb filled their nostrils and made their mouths water.

'What was going on?' they wondered. The household had been so subdued and sombre for weeks and now by contrast there was this atmosphere of celebration. They were astonished to see so many smiling friends gathered together eating, drinking, and laughing. Their eyes sought out their mother who was beaming, her face full of joy and her eyes sparkling with happiness. Mary weaved her way through the crowd, holding out her arms to welcome them.

"Come and see, your brother is home. Isn't it wonderful? He is so looking forward to seeing you all."

Bemused, they followed their mother through the garden to the fig tree –her favourite spot, where her eldest son was seated. Upon seeing him they stopped short in their tracks. The last time they had seen him, he was dirty, dishevelled, streaked with blood, humiliated, and shaking with fear. Now he sat facing them, clean in body and clothing, his straggly hair and beard had been trimmed and washed, his already olive skin had been darkened by the sun and the wind. Although he was thinner, his body looked muscular and strong. He smiled at them and his eyes crinkled with happiness. Whereas before, they had sent out bolts of fire and brimstone, now his eyes signalled a calmness and peace, reinforced with determination. Even his voice was different, deeper and reassuring as he stood and greeted them. He had had a small child on his lap, his sister's daughter, whom he gave a gentle hug, a kiss on her cheek, and handed her back to her mother.

"I have come to make my peace with you," he said quietly and embraced each of them. They in turn hugged him and slapped him on the back, except Joseph, who stiffened and did not return the gesture of love and friendship. Instead he turned away abruptly and found his mother.

"What is all this about?" he demanded angrily. "Why the party? He is the one who left in disgrace, who hardly ever did a hand's turn to provide for the family. He's the one who turned his back on us. We stayed and worked. We put up with the accusations and abuse from the priests when he was run out of the village. We're the ones who had to face the neighbours – not him. You never gave a party for us to show your appreciation. Now this… it's like you don't even recognize our efforts to look after you!"

Mary reacted to his outburst as though he had slapped her face.

"Oh Joseph!" she cried wringing her hands and close to tears. "Don't say such things. You know I love you all dearly. You are here every day, I see you and know you are safe and well. You all have good, settled lives and I hope you are contented. But him, he has been lost and unsure of himself for so long. He has been looking, without success, for a meaning in his life. When he went away I was afraid that I would never see him again. When he came back into the house this morning I hardly recognized him. I don't mean his bedraggled appearance. He has changed so much. He is confident, purposeful and self-assured but not in a bragging, rumbustious way. He is happy and at peace with himself. He knows now what he is going to do with his life. He won't be with us for very long, so please, just enjoy having him home and thank God that he is safe and well."

Joseph shrugged his shoulders and turned away. He was not easily persuaded to forgive his brother and still burned with resentment. However, as everyone else seemed to have forgotten the reason for his brother leaving home, he decided to put aside his jealousy for the moment and enjoy the spread that his mother had worked so hard to provide.

James, meanwhile, was listening intently to his brother's account of his weeks in the wilderness, the temptations he had endured and his plans for the future. Both men seemed oblivious to their surroundings. Being a very devout Jew, James found a little difficulty in accepting his brother's new ideas of modifying or changing the way in which he and many others observed the laws of Moses and how they traditionally worshipped God.

"I am ready to accept that the Kingdom of God is coming very soon," he said gravely. "The time is right. I pray every day for deliverance from the Romans and the restoration of Israel to the Jewish people. I understand that prayer is not enough and that we must take some responsibility to fulfil God's wishes and the Prophesies. The trouble is how to achieve these aims. As you say, bloodshed is not God's way. The underground movements, hit and run outbursts, can never in the long run overcome the might of Rome. We've talked about it for many hours in the synagogue without a solution. Your way sounds much better – if it is possible. My problem is you. You are my brother whom I have grown up with, played and tumbled with all my life. How can I now accept now that you are the son of God? Teacher? – yes rabbi, leader, prophet all those things are possible, but that you are one and the same as Him I find hard to believe." James' eyes were full of doubt. He loved his brother very much but saw him as a man, one who was special and different, although still a human being.

"I would like to be part of your mission, to help in any way I can. Maybe Jude would agree to becoming one of your band of followers too." He looked up with a new determined light in his eyes. "Give me a few days to think about it and I will see you in Capernaum, along with Jude if he is willing. I don't think there is any chance of Joseph joining us. He is too wrapped up in his work here. Mother will be glad if we are together. She will see us from time to time as we will be only a couple of day's walk away"

Their discussion was interrupted by loud wailing sound. Their sister, Salome's daughter, had fallen bumping her head and grazing her arm. Although Salome tried to hug her and kiss her better, the little girl would have none of it. She lifted her little tear stained face to look at her favourite uncle, pouted her quivering bottom lip and raised her podgy arms towards him.

James said, "Don't take any notice. the women will sort her out."

But he brushed James aside saying, "Let her come to me. She trusts me and believes I will help her. If only everyone was as innocent as this child my work would be easy." He reached for the child, gave her a big reassuring smile and gently pressed two fingers onto her forehead and his other hand on her arm. He closed his eyes and seemed to whisper some inaudible words under his breath. Immediately her sobs ceased, the redness of the bump disappeared and there was no sign of injury on her plump little arm. She clapped her hands and giggled, her pain forgotten as she enjoyed being the centre of attention. Everyone marvelled at her quick recovery amazed that there was no sign of her ever having been hurt.

"It's a miracle!" said one.

"I've heard of healing by the laying on of hands," said another.

"Did he really do it, or are we seeing things?" wondered a third.

"He did it alright. I wonder if he could cure the pains in my legs. They are so bad I can hardly stand in the mornings!"

The conversation buzzed back and forth round the guests and family. What news they would be able to pass on to their families and neighbours when they got home!

James watched their animated faces and listened to their chattering voices. There was no doubt in his mind that his brother had healed the child and if this was so easy, he thought, what else could he achieve? He decided there and then to set his affairs in order and journey to Capernaum to be part of his brother's group of close followers. Would his brother Jude come with him? He had no idea what lay ahead but a burst of excitement ran through him. Something monumental was about to happen and he would be a part of it.

CHAPTER SEVEN

The Road To Capernaum

He left his home village of Nazareth a few days later with a light heart and a spring in his step not knowing, or caring, if he would ever return. They had spurned him, disbelieving that one of their own could possibly be the Son of God as he had once claimed. The messiah was coming alright but he would be a political leader or a warrior fit to claim the throne of David they believed, not the son of the local carpenter and not even that, if old rumours were to be believed.

The narrow, dusty track was quiet at this hour of the day. Most of the villagers were at their work in the fields so he had time to think and plan his journey as he walked along. He carried little; some bread, dates, figs, a few shekels and a goatskin pouch of water. He wore clean new clothes and comfortable leather sandals; well-oiled so they would not crack from the dry, dusty sand beneath his feet.

Eventually the track merged with a busy road which was the main highway leading to Jerusalem in Judea and on to Egypt and Arabia in the south. Northwards the road lead to Tiberius and Capernaum, winding through Galilee, Caesarea Philippi and even further along the trade routes to Damascus and Syria. Merchant caravans plied their trade up and down this highway often travelling in large numbers to avoid attacks by marauding bandits. Strangers were often welcomed to join them so they could share news, gossip and discuss the philosophy of the day. Most were wealthy, speaking smatterings of several languages, Hebrew, Aramaic, Greek, Roman and Arabic all necessary to carry out their business and reflecting the legacies of the various occupations by oppressors over the last century. Other traders were not so hospitable, singularly interested in reaching the next town or city, sell their goods and make as big a profit as possible, buy more stocks usually from the locals as cheaply as possible and return home to count their money.

Occasionally the merchants had to move their carts, camels, oxen and donkeys rapidly to the side of the road to allow the passage of a troupe of Roman soldiers in their chariots or on horseback, their plumed helmets and breastplates glistening in the sun, kicking up a storm of dust as they thundered past.

"Always in a hurry these Romans," grumbled one of the merchants. "If we don't get out of the way fast enough, our carts and animals get cut down by the spikes on their chariot wheels and they don't care one iota!"

Within a couple of hours the caravan arrived at the city of Sepphorus. Built by the Greeks less than a hundred years ago and added to by the Romans it was one of the ten new cities known as Decapolis. In contrast to the rural surroundings, it was a beautiful modern place to live. Palatial homes with pillars and statues, shady courtyards and ornate mosaics adorning the floors and walls. Not only Romans inhabited these grand buildings, many nationalities made their home there, including rich Hebrew families who emulated the foreigners' lifestyles, much to the annoyance of their more orthodox compatriots.

In the centre of the city there were great open spaces used for social gatherings and marketing goods from all over the known world. Silks, spices such as frankincense, often burned by priests to rid the synagogue of the smell of charred meat and blood of sacrifices, woollen cloth, wood carvings, ornaments, household goods as well as locally produced fruit and wine.

Artisans had premises where they made and sold their wares. Ornate copper trays, platters and jugs were manufactured next door to the potter spinning his wheel and moulding his wet clay into pots and containers of all shapes and sizes. Carpenters sawed, chiselled and polished furniture. Tallow bubbled in vats to make candles and lamps. Stonemasons hammered and chipped at blocks of granite or sandstone for even more building work. Ostlers, dyers, weavers, bakers, peddlers, money changers, scribes all added to the colour, hustle and bustle of everyday life.

After dark the local brothel was kept busy and prosperous. Traders and merchants passing through or the soldiers from the local garrison made up the majority of customers. Prostitution was commonplace in the cities, the women were often country girls, foreigners or those who were widowed or turned out by their husbands and had to make a living in order to eat.

Disease was rife. Although the Romans brought knowledge of aqueducts and supplies of fresh water there was little of it for the poor who used wells or the rivers for washing, bathing or drinking. Foreign travellers brought many types of infection against which most people had little or no immunity. Life expectancy was short, medical aid was poor or non-existent. Alongside the richness there sat poverty, disease, rubbish, sewage, begging, thieving and helplessness all of which was ignored by society, the majority of whom counted their blessings that they were not so afflicted.

As the man walked through the busy streets, he remembered the sights, sounds and smells from when he was a boy. He had visited with his father, Joseph, to sell his furniture, take commissions or work in the new houses. His mother came too to sell fine woollen cloth she had made at home and dyed in vibrant colours she had made from vegetable and fruit sources.

He passed a boy dressed in rags, bearing his weight on roughly hewn crutches, his swollen foot wrapped tightly in dirty cloth tied with thin, frayed rope. His eyes were blank as he held out his hand for alms. His young life was miserable and held no hope for the future. He was surprised when the traveller turned back to him, gave him some bread and a few dates, then, casting a glance up and down the road, took hold of his crutches. The boy was about to call out but was caught in the man's gaze. Undoing the filthy rags the man quietly said

"You don't need crutches anymore. Your foot is healed and strong. Go home and help your family."

Amazed, the boy looked at his foot. The swelling had gone as had the infection and the bones felt whole, causing him no pain as he tested his weight on it. He looked up to speak to the stranger but there was no one, he had gone, disappearing into the crowds. With a whoop he kicked his crutches away and ran off, eager to tell his family what had happened!

Later that day the man made his way to the synagogue to pray. As he crossed the area reserved for women he observed a lady dressed in black on her knees fervently praying, hands clasped with tears rolling down her lined cheeks,

Probably a widow, he thought. Life will be pretty hard for her if she has no one to support her. She scratched in her worn bag for a few coins, clutching them tightly as though reluctant to let them go, then she stood and dropped them in the box which fed the coffers of the synagogue. A nearby Pharisee observed the paltry contribution, and with a disdainful look he poured several shekels into the box, thinking how much more good his contribution would do than that of the bedraggled old biddy.

The man shook his head and thought, Her gift pleases God much more than the rich man's and it cost her a lot more than his self-satisfied gesture did. He turned on his heel and walked away. He would pray in his own way. He did not need arrogant lay priests to tell him how to worship God or to interpret the scriptures for him. He would pray for both of them to understand that it is better to please God than themselves.

Later as he sat in the courtyard of the small inn where he was staying the night, he ate a meal of bread and barley broth with a little boiled lamb. By the light of the fire he observed his fellow guests. One or two were merchants still haggling and bargaining, others were settling down for the night having fed themselves and their animals they prepared to sleep on piles of straw covered in rugs and blankets.

A small group of men sat in a corner of the courtyard, drinking wine, talking over the events of the day and throwing dice. The gambling was mainly good humoured until one man lost heavily and started accusing the others of cheating. The argument became heated, loud and then physical. Blows were being traded until the innkeeper, a burly ox of a man who had no truck with scrapping ruffians appeared. He quickly separated the main protagonists, held them at arm's length and told them they were no longer welcome. Grabbing a handful of money, the loser quickly departed and disappeared into the night. The others massaged their bruised knuckles and sore heads, shared out the coins which were left muttering curses under their breath and also called it a night. Tomorrow was another day. business as usual but for now, back to their lodgings or home to nagging wives demanding money for food, clothing, trinkets or their daughter's dowry.

As he sat, he thought about the day. It had been all about money. Making it, changing it, counting it, gambling it and losing it. Money, it seemed was all people cared about whether they had a lot or a little. No doubt it would be the same in other big towns or cities. Money here was king not God. He doubted that his message would find roots in places like this. There were too many other things to worship. Too many nationalities and different beliefs, even most of the Jewish community only paid lip service to their religion. Demands of the unbelievers made it difficult to observe the laws of the Sabbath. Could Judaism survive the pluralistic society where there seemed to be no rules of worship? Some who could not tolerate this way of life fled the cities for fear of persecution and formed bands of insurgents nipping at the heels of the Romans causing even more unrest and uncertainty in the country. He decided that his mission, if it was to be successful would be carried out amongst the simple folk of the countryside until there was a groundswell big enough for the rulers and city folk to sit up and take notice.

Closing his eyes and mind he slept, dreaming of nothing but the smiling face of Mara, her twinkling eyes, copper curls blowing in the wind and the tingle of her lips on his. The next morning he rose early and broke his fast with bread, goat's cheese and milk. He left the city and shook off the dirt from his feet, glad to be away from the smells and clamour, once more striding out with purpose and resolution.

He left the main road, preferring the country lanes and tracks. Sometimes he was given a ride on an ox cart to a village where he taught in the local meeting house if there was no synagogue or the in shade of a tree or at the home of a fellow traveller. They shared their food with him and he in return, healed their sick children, elderly parents, friends and neighbours, always invoking God's help. He told stories about the love of God, strengthened their faith and if there was a river or stream nearby he baptized them as his cousin John had done.

They were amazed at this remarkable man who was so gentle, patient and utterly believable. Word soon spread that there was a new healer in the area, a new rabbi and soon quite a crowd joined him on the road, eager to see, hear and touch him. They told him their own stories and asked him questions such as,

"When is the kingdom of God coming?" to which he replied,

"Maybe not in my life time, but soon. So, repent of your sins, be born again by being baptized and let there be no more wrong doing."

The people he met were mainly hard-working, honest souls who just wanted a decent life for their families. They tended their crops or animals, built their own dwellings and observed the Sabbath. One man, however confessed that a couple of his sheep had gone missing, wandered off in the night and he had gone looking for them.

"I didn't want them getting lost or being stolen by bandits. We have little enough and need the wool and meat even though it is forbidden to work or walk so far on the Sabbath." He was comforted when the man told him that God would not be angry with him for saving the sheep. It showed that he cared for them and that the Sabbath was made for man's benefit, not the other way round.

If, at the end of the day, he was nowhere near a village he would seek shelter in a cave, glad of the solitude to pray, think and regain his strength. People pressed against him and wanted so much from him that he sometimes felt physically and mentally drained, needing the peace and quiet to rest and prepare for the task ahead.

As he walked he surveyed the fields and terraced vineyards. Some areas were large, others small. It was customary for an owner to divide his land between his sons, so over the generations the plots became smaller. Some were well worked and productive, others where the ground was stony the land was barren and almost useless for growing anything. Many of the owners had to sell parts of their land to pay taxes or take the consequences at the hands of the unforgiving Romans. If they were lucky they sold to a neighbour who would keep them on working as labourers, although with only a pittance of a wage. The not so lucky had to sell everything try to find work, rely on friends and family for survival or beg at the side of the road. These were desperate times. Only the belief that the Messiah was coming gave them hope. The good times were just round the corner. Was this stranger, who healed and taught that the Kingdom of God was at hand the One, they wondered?

He grasped the enormity of what he was promising and prayed diligently that, with God's help, he was up to the task and would deliver.

I must find some help and soon, he thought. It is too big a task to do alone.

Skirting the garrison town of Tiberius, he walked instead along the shore of the Sea of Galilee, gazing in wonderment at the dark, imposing Golan Heights at the opposite side of the water. He had no desire to spend time in the city, preferring to feel the wind on his face, the lapping of the waves and listening to the banter of the fishermen as they mended their nets and sails. A good catch of fine, fat silver fish was being loaded into a cart before being hauled off to the Migdahl towers for salting or smoking.

He remembered Mara talking about the towers her father owned for preserving the fish and decided to visit the family to tell her of the progress he had made. As he approached he first saw the smoke and smelled the sweetness of the charring cedar wood from the towers. He passed areas flooded with water of varying depths evaporating in the sun, leaving a residue of salt, water brought courtesy of Archimedes' screw into ditches, by a shadduf or a waterwheel powered by a patient donkey. Layers of salt crusted and glistened in the sunshine. Everyone knew the home of the Migdahlenes. They caught fish for them, hauled, smoked, salted or sold fish for them. Everyone in the village was connected to them in some way.

He arrived at the house, a very grand building, and was about to introduce himself to Maryam's father when she came flying across the courtyard, her long headdress billowing out behind her like the sails of a ship.

"I thought it might be you" she gushed, resisting the urge to throw her arms round him. "I heard that a stranger was asking for us. How wonderful to see you again." Turning to her bewildered father she explained, "He's the one I told you about. You remember little Yeshi? Joseph and Mary's son from Nazareth? You just haven't seen him in many years."

Her father's eyes lit up with recognition and memories.

"Of course I remember Yeshi. My, how the years have flown past!" He then ushered his visitor inside to eat supper with them and catch up on all the news. Maryam had told him of the wonderful journeys he had taken and after a seemingly aimless life he had finally settled down to become a rabbi. There were other things she had not told him, things that perhaps he was not yet ready to understand.

'Yavas, Yeshi', she thought. 'Slowly'. He nodded his agreement as though she had spoken aloud.

They sat many hours together, the guest explaining his plans in more detail. Maryam served them supper, a feast of bread, roasted lamb on a spit, fish, cheese fruit and wine from the local vineyard. She left them to continue talking further into the night. Eventually, they prayed together before sleeping in the upper rooms now cooled by the breeze from the sea.

He woke at daybreak to find a pile of clean clothes to wear and after washing in water from a nearby well he felt suitably rested and refreshed and keen to be on his way. He prayed that he might find the right people to follow him and gave thanks that he had made so many good friends along the way. Supplied with more than enough food to sustain him on the last stage of his journey, he wished them well and prepared to leave when Mara tugged his sleeve.

"I have a present for you," she whispered, smiling. She took him to a large workroom at the back of the house where two women were weaving cloth and another was carding wool. "I told you I had my own business," she said proudly, "and I made this specially for you."

Puzzled he took the bundle of dark red, lightweight cloth from her and shook it out. It was the finest robe he had ever seen, so soft and warm. Mara laughed out loud.

"It is made from the finest wool from the throats of many sheep. I made it all myself and dyed it from the juice of berries from the mountains."

His eyes shone with pleasure as he handled the material. "It is beautiful Mara, fit for a king. What a wonderful woman you are. Thank you." He reached out and kissed her, much to the amusement of the other women. Mara cast down her eyes and blushed, pleased by the embrace.

Outside once more he mounted the donkey, lent to him by Mara's father for the rest of the way as it was half a day's journey, longer on foot. Promising to return the animal as soon as possible, he smiled, waved goodbye clutching his precious bundle. Mara, pretending to tighten the rope holding the water carrier, pressed her arm against him and whispered, "Careful Yeshi. Think of me until we meet again soon Send me your thoughts, I will be listening."

He looked down, his dark brown eyes conveying the message she wanted to hear, then he waved one last time, wheeled his donkey and was gone. She stood and watched until he was just a dot on the road then obscured altogether by a cloud of dust. A great sadness came over her. 'Is this how it will end Yeshi?' she thought. 'You disappearing in a cloud'. Suddenly her heart was heavy.

CHAPTER EIGHT

The Fisherman

As he approached Capernaum, a small town on the northern shores of the Sea of Galilee, he became aware of two men following him. He was used to people joining him on his travels but this was different, moving when he moved, stopping when he stopped and hastily looking away if he turned to see them. He sighed and slowly dismounted. "Why are you following me?" he called out.

The elder of the two, a large, broad shouldered man with greying hair and muscular arms gave him a sideways glance and called back

"You're him, aren't you? You're the one we've been waiting for." The other man, presumably the younger brother as he had the same features cut in.

"We saw you that day in the Jordan when you were baptized. We were followers of John and he told us you were the one to come after him, that you were greater than him and that we should follow you to do God's work."

He smiled and said, "Then walk with me and we will talk."

The brothers, called Simon and Andrew, were fishermen who owned a small warehouse near Bethsaida along the coast from Capernaum. They were not rich, their boat was small and leaky but well patched and tarred. They were not very well educated but were honest and sincere in their love of God. By the time they reached Capernaum quite a crowd had gathered, curious to see this new preacher they had heard about. They were mainly fishermen mending their nets ready for the next sailing and local townsfolk.

There were too many to see or hear him properly so he asked Simon to row him out a little way in his boat. He began to speak and the crowd settled down to listen. He talked about the prophets and how Isaiah had promised that the people of this area would be the first to see the great light, that the Kingdom of God is coming soon, that they should repent, be baptized to be reborn and that he would show them the way. He then gave them God's blessing and sank down into the boat, tired but exhilarated. "Let's go fishing," he said to which Simon shook his head. "We were working all night and hardly caught a thing."

"Trust me," he said fixing them with his gaze. "You won't regret it." Shrugging, Simon and Andrew pulled out further to sea and cast their net wide. After a while they began to pull it in again, surprised to find it was remarkably heavy going.

"If we try to lift this lot, the net will break and we will lose everything," Andrew panted, his arms straining with effort. Simon looked to shore, spotted two of his friends, again two brothers, fishermen like himself and called out to them, "James, John, get yourselves over here. Bring your nets and help us haul in the catch; just wait 'til you see it." Along with their father, Zebedee, the brothers quickly came alongside and with great effort together they managed to land the enormous catch. Amazed, John shouted to everyone to come, look and share their good fortune. Used to shouting above the noise of the wind and flapping sails, John's voice was booming. "We call him 'The Thunderer'," laughed Andrew. "'Cause you can hear him for miles!"

Simon turned to thank the man, not just for the fish but for giving them a sign. Nodding, the man gazed at them earnestly. "Leave your catch and your boat. Follow me and I will make you fishers of men." Without hesitation Simon answered, "No problem, Its old and leaky anyway. Andrew and I have been waiting for you and we're ready. Let's go home and have supper. Stay with us and tell us more."

Upon reaching home, Simon called out to his mother. His wife came out and shushed him. "Your mother is sick, Simon. She has had a fever for days." When he heard this the man went to Simon's mother's room. Her eyes were red and her lips were dry although a fine sheen of sweat glistened on her forehead. He took her hand firmly, closed his eyes and called upon God to take the fever away. After a couple of minutes her breathing steadied and the fever left her. She sighed and sat up.

"I feel so much better", she said, "but I'm starving! Let me go and see about some supper." Everyone marvelled at her bustling about her kitchen, humming to herself. She did indeed serve them all a meal, putting everyone in a good mood.

"How did you do that?" asked Andrew.

"It was God's work," he replied, "and I will teach you how to do it along with so many more things."

The following morning as they set out for the synagogue, they met up with brothers James and John. "We have been talking half the night," boomed James. He was a tall, well-built man, with short black hair and a thick beard. In contrast, his much younger brother was slight of stature, smooth skinned, had a handsome face and sparkling eyes. "And we have decided to come with you."

"If you'll have us," interjected John. "We want to learn more"

"Goes without sayin'," carried on James. "Our father will carry on the business, no problem. It is far more important to spread the news God's Kingdom is coming soon."

He answered, "Yesterday you helped your friends without question. I gladly welcome you to join me. It will not always be easy, but people will certainly hear that booming voice of yours James!" He clasped both their hands, happy to have found willing recruits so easily. He stayed in Capernaum several more days and decided to make it his base. He was amongst friends, could heal the sick, preach, baptize and teach his new followers to do things in God's name.

As promised, he turned his face southwards once again, to attend the wedding in Cana. His mother was organizing the feast after the marriage ceremony as the bridegroom's mother, who had been Mary's best friend since childhood, had died some years earlier. She was in her element fluttering round seeing that everything was perfect. Maryam and her father were also attending the wedding and she managed to slip away for a few minutes with Yeshi. It proved difficult as so many people wanted to talk to him and ask him questions but was eventually rewarded. She commented on his wearing of his new cloak which many people had admired. Then they talked of his mission and the four new disciples. "How many do you want Yeshi?" she asked.

"Ideally twelve," he replied. "This is symbolic of the twelve tribes of Israel. Everything is to re-enforce the message. Any more would not easily be managed."

"Think carefully who you choose Yeshi," she warned. "You have four fishermen without much education. Look for people you can trust, of course, but try to find them in as many different walks of life as you can" She paused then went on. "In fact, I may have someone for you. He is a good friend of mine called Phillip. His family came from Egypt with us all those years ago. He's a thinker, a good organizer, speaks several languages and is a seeker after truth."

"He sounds too good to be true." He laughed. "Where will I find this paragon of virtue?"

"I'm not joking!" she snapped back. "He's a good man, you'll really like him. Go and speak to him at least." Then, hastily because she saw his mother approaching with a frown on her face, urged him, "Tomorrow, next village. Be there!" Turning to Mary she asked with concern, "What's the matter? You look as though something dreadful has happened."

"Disaster," she gasped looking pointedly at her son. "The wine has run out and nobody is showing signs of going home yet"

"Why are you telling me?" he asked.

"Because you can do something about it. You know you can," she stated flatly.

Glancing round awkwardly, he muttered between clenched teeth ,"I don't want to get involved. My time has not yet come."

Dismissing his protest with a toss of her head, she called to one of the servants saying "Do whatever he tells you – no questions asked."

Near the courtyard gateway stood several large stone vats of clean water ready for the guests to wash their hands before leaving. The servant was told to take a jug, fill it with water and serve it to his master. Looking sceptical he did so, half expecting his master to box his ears or throw him out. Instead his master called out to the bridegroom, "Hey Ari, this wine is excellent. Why have you kept it 'til last? It should have come first so we could really appreciate it. Loch Chaim!" Everyone laughed and continued drinking the wine well into the night. The servant was amazed at this miraculous event and told the other servants what had happened, he looked for Mary's son but the man had gone.

Maryam and the brothers met up with the man the next morning and they set off back on the road to Capernaum once more. Walking through a small village they saw children playing, women milking goats or grinding corn, a man sitting under a fig tree and another scrutinizing a scroll of papyrus.

"That's him... Phillip," whispered Maryam nudging him towards the scholarly looking man, deep in thought.

"What are you studying my friend?" he asked.

Phillip sighed. "I'm trying to find the answer to what has gone wrong with our religion and our people. There is so much confusion, law breaking and complacency these days. I can't find the way forward in the scriptures. I'm in despair."

"Then follow me and together we will make the changes," the man said. Phillip looked long and deeply into the stranger's eyes then nodded.

"Yes," he said. "I sense you are the one with the vision, the will and the strength to do it. You are the Nazarene aren't you? Wait and I will call my friend." Turning he walked a little way down the road and called, "Nathanial! This is the man Moses predicted would come. He's from Nazareth. Come and talk to him."

"Nothing good ever came from Nazareth," Nathanial grunted but lifted himself from the seat in the shade. As he approached, the stranger remarked, "Here comes a true Israelite, a good man with nothing evil in him."

"You know nothing about me!" retorted Nathanial.

"I passed you earlier under the fig tree before I even saw Phillip and was immediately aware of your character and goodness. You are just the sort of man I am looking for. Join us," invited the man. As Phillip had done earlier, Nathanial studied the man's face and felt the power in his gaze. "Yes rabbi, I will come with you because you have been sent by God to restore Israel." The man clapped him on the back and said incredulously, "You believe in me simply because I saw you under the fig tree? I will show you greater things in the future my friend, even heaven itself."

The growing band of followers once more set out for Capernaum, talking, listening and questioning each other. Before reaching the town they split into pairs with instructions to spread the word as far and as quickly as possible. "Tell people what you know, what you believe. Even do baptisms. Give them their faith back. Don't worry about food, people will feed you and give you shelter. Meet back at Peter's house in a few days"

He and Maryam walked on together, holding hands and talking about their latest recruits. "You're halfway there, Yeshi. Another six to find and you're in business. I've been busy too, getting round my friends, telling them about you – not in too much detail of course and they are all willing to help." She proceeded to list them, some of whom he knew already, others he would meet in the future. "Mary of Bethany, she's the sister of Martha and Lazarus, Suzannah, she's very rich and will give money, food and shelter to anyone of you in the area. Then there's Joanna," she continued, hardly pausing for breath, "she's the wife of Herod's chief steward and hears loads of gossip."

He laughed but was pleased at her enthusiasm. "You have been busy, Mara. You are so kind and generous, we will want for nothing. As usual you are very good for me. What would I do without you?"

"You don't have to… Do without me I mean. I'll come and see you whenever I can. I want to help and learn too." She hesitated. "As well as being with you as often as possible."

He held her close for a long time. "Come when you can Mara. I will be busy but my thoughts will be with you. I need to go now. Pray for me as I will pray for you." They kissed one last time and she turned away quickly to hide her tears.

Over the next few weeks they each travelled far and wide, preaching in streets, houses, on hilltops, the seashore, anywhere people would listen. They converted many and baptized them, some rejected them saying they were rabble rousers and turned away. They even went into the network of caves in the cliffs above the Sea of Galilee where the zealots hid. Led by Barabbas who organized and carried out hit and run raids against the Romans. He was seen by many to be a freedom fighter and liberator, so he was much loved as a hero. A few of his men however, although keen to be rid of the hated army of oppressors, were sickened by all the bloodshed and the crucifixions which followed by way of retribution. One such man was called Simon. He was determined to help restore Israel to the Jewish people. As soon as he heard the new rabbi teaching, he knew that this peaceful, non-political, non-violent approach was the way forward. He immediately joined the rabbi's followers to learn more and was keen to help.

The leader of the group, now called rabbi, teacher, or master, stayed mainly round Capernaum, preaching but also looking for other converts to join his inner circle. He found some in unlikely circumstances. One day whilst walking through the market place, he came across a man sitting at the tax collector's table. Most people hated and reviled tax collectors. Not only were they Jews working for the Romans, extracting the onerous dues but they also added their own percentage on the top thus becoming rich at the expense of their neighbours. This man's name was Matthew and was regarded as an extortionist, seeming to delight in other people's misery and hardship. He had no friends except other tax collectors and traders who were also hated because of their Roman connections and grasping lifestyles. Many had abandoned the laws of Moses, making the excuse that their customers did not observe the Sabbath so they were forced to work on that day.

The man walked up to the table and said, "There is a way of life more rewarding than this. Follow me and I will show you the glory of the kingdom of heaven, the love of God is worth far more than you earn on earth." Matthew stood up and without saying a word, he left his table and took the man home to eat and rest. He was amazed at the stranger's attitude towards him. This man understood what Matthew was really like underneath the veneer. He decided to join the group saying, "If God can forgive a man like me, He can forgive anyone." Not everyone welcomed the new addition to the team and some of the people who had listened to the rabbi teaching began to have doubts.

"Why does he eat and stay at the house of such sinners?" they questioned. The rabbi understood their concerns and said, "The righteous do not need reminding about God. It is these very sinners who need help to change their ways."

The most ardent and sincere of his many followers were willing to give up their employment, home ties and leave their possessions behind to be with him. Convinced that one day soon God would reclaim his lands and people. Somehow, miraculously, the Roman 'problem' would disappear. He had spent much time with them and knew all their strengths and weaknesses. One had stood out from the rest. Young, tall and strong he came from Karioth and was named Judas. He crackled with energy and enthusiasm. There was fire in his belly and light in his eyes. He had been a radical, even more zealous than Simon. He was a member of a group of men who followed the example of Yehuda Maccabeus, nicknamed 'The Hammer' a leader of an insurgency against the enemy over a century ago. This group of angry young men was called Sicarii or 'Dagger men' Judas had heard that this new leader was gathering converts as quickly as possible, claiming that the Kingdom of God would be restored within a generation. Convinced that when the numbers were great enough this new

'Hammer' would strike and retake Jerusalem, he fervently and devoutly offered his services.

The number of regular followers had swelled to about one hundred and new converts were arriving every day. There were too many now to meet in houses or market squares so mostly they gathered on a hillside just out of town overlooking the sea. It was where he taught, preached and gave his blessing. It was also where he retreated to rest, think and commune with God. The group was becoming unwieldy and it was time to select his core of twelve, choices had to be made. He thought long and hard about who to choose and prayed to God that he made the right decision. He walked a little way from the gathered crowd one morning, until all could see and hear him. He made a short speech saying that he would name the twelve chosen by God to be the new sons of Jacob, who they knew symbolized love and hope as well as the twelve tribes of Israel. Although he would only name twelve there was much work to be done by the others with God's help and blessing. He called out the names of those to stand beside him.

"Simon, Andrew, James, John, Phillip, Nathanial and Matthew." There was a gasp from the crowd at this choice but he continued, "Simon the zealot, Thomas, his brother James and James' son Thaddeus and finally…" He paused and thoughts flashed through his mind, is this right? Am I sure? Is he the special one? He cleared his throat and announced clearly, "…and finally, Judas of Karioth. You are all my new brothers, my family God be praised." To the others he said, "Go in peace, do God's work and together we will not fail."

His mother Mary and his brothers were amongst the crowd. She was surprised and a little disappointed that he had not chosen James or Jude to be included in the twelve, if only to keep an eye on him. She did not like this collection he called his 'brothers' and 'family', they were too radical. However,

James and Jude were good men and would continue to do what they could.

Even Maryam and her friend Suzannah who had brought food and money for the men, felt a little sceptical. "Such a diverse group of people, how will he keep control and track of what they are all doing?" Once again she felt concern in the pit of her stomach.

"Careful Yeshi, be alert, There are people out there who would do you harm." She fixed his back with her gaze and sent him her thoughts. He turned to look at her as he walked down the hillside, "I hear you Mara, but don't worry. I know what I am doing," he silently replied.

CHAPTER NINE

The Teacher

Over the next few months a pattern developed for the disciples' new way of life. They made their base in the caves above Capernaum where they stored food and wine given to them by their families, friends and villagers. It was their temporary home where they lived, slept, learned and prayed. Going out into the communities, usually in pairs, they ventured far and wide in each direction, to Tyre and Sidon, Jericho and Judea, sometimes even through Samaria. In the early days the master would go with them, teaching by example. They watched, listened and learned many things from him, developing their own skills and style.

They usually travelled four days each week, preaching the word of God, baptizing and telling people about the new leader, asking them to come and listen to him for themselves. When they were not travelling they shared their experiences, good and bad, were taught new skills and learned more from the master. Not everyone was away at the same time, so there was always someone at their cave home.

The master withdrew further up the hillside occasionally so he could find solitude, refresh his spirit, reflect on his progress and pray to God for guidance, always thinking, What next? How does that fit in with the overall plan? He had not revealed his total plan, not even to Mara, but was developing it slowly bit by bit. On the Sabbath everyone rested according to the law.

Some of the disciples could hardly read or write, never having had the need to do so. Phillip and Nathanial helped them by teaching the basic skills. They also made notes of the master's teachings so that they could remind themselves later. Judas taught them how to defend themselves should they be attacked by thieves. The carrying of weapons was banned by the Romans, but every one of them carried an implement of some sort, a knife used for gutting fish, or butchering a sheep, a sling and pebbles to ward off animals, something to whittle wood or chisel stone, they were all weapons of a kind. Judas had learned how to sharpen his sicar, or razor, to be used as a dagger, which is why his former friends were known as 'sicarii'.

They sat for hours in the morning sun, in the shade at noon or by a fire at night listening, learning and asking questions. As he had learned many years before the master answered their questions by telling a story and ending with a question of his own. This was the way many of them had learned the scriptures as children so they understood the method and applied it to their own way of teaching. Sometimes they were dispirited and frustrated, especially when a whole village refused to listen to them and maybe even spat on them. "What do we do?" asked Matthew. "Keep trying?"

"No!" bellowed James. "Send a thunderbolt from God! Wipe 'em all out."

"Typical answer," muttered Andrew under his breath. The master told the story of seeds falling on stony ground, how it would never produce a crop no matter how many times the farmer tried. "Better to find fertile land and have the seed produce a hundredfold at harvest. Turn your back on those who refuse to listen, your words are wasted."

As they developed their understanding, the rabbi taught the disciples in more direct ways. He showed them which herbs or leaves from the hedgerows could be sued to heal sores or cool fevers. He taught healing by the laying on of hands and calling for God's help, casting out demons, meditation and how to pray to God. He gave them many examples of parables to illustrate their own teaching. They asked him how to describe the Kingdom of Heaven and he told them it was like planting the tiniest of seeds and watching it grow into the largest plant they had ever seen, so big that even the birds wanted to nest in it. "This means," he explained, "that something wonderful and different is coming something beyond our understanding."

Maryam often joined them, learned alongside them all the skills and wisdom. She asked more questions than anyone, was quick to understand and could often answer the disciples' questions herself. Some of them did not like her being there. Other women, friends, wives and family came to the cave to bring food, supplies of clean clothing and gifts of money but Maryam was the only one who joined the teaching sessions. Simon was particularly annoyed at her presence. Not only because she was a woman and not one of the chosen twelve but because of the special relationship developing between herself and the master. Sometimes they sat and ate apart from the others, talking and laughing together. He saw that they sometimes held hands and delighted in each other's company. She walked with the master in front of all the others when she should know her place and walk behind.

One evening a question was asked about visions. Maryam, remembering her experience in the wilderness, quickly jumped in with the answer.

This was too much for Simon. He burst out angrily, "Have you been talking with this woman behind our backs? Tell her to leave. Some women are not worthy of life, let alone the kingdom of God!" A stunned silence descended on the group. The man looked sad and sighed.

"Simon," he said quietly controlling his own anger, "you of all people should trust me. You were the first one I chose and are the bedrock for my work. As for Mara, whose very name means 'teacher', I have known her since childhood. Of course I have spoken to her privately. Everyone has the right to ask questions. When women see the light and understand what I am saying, then they become like men and can enter the Kingdom of God. Men, women and children, those that have ears to listen, let them hear. God does not pick and choose. We are all His children." Simon withdrew from the group further into the cave, still simmering but pleased to hear that he was chosen to be the bedrock of the campaign. He decided not to be in the same place as Maryam and to hold his tongue in his master's hearing.

Another disciple, emboldened by Simon's approach asked, "Why do you love her more than all of us?" to which the master replied in his usual questioning manner. "Think. Why do I NOT love you as I love her?"

Phillip sat quietly at the rear of the group, keeping his thoughts to himself. He knew the very name Migdahl meant 'tower' or 'elevated', 'great or 'magnificent'. His thoughts turned to his linguistic skills and in his mind he changed the Hebrew word for 'companion' into Greek which also meant 'consort'. Not only had he witnessed the holding of hands but also he had seen their leader kissing Maryam, not in the usual way of greeting but full on the lips in a passionate embrace. He was not offended in any way since it was unusual for a man of the rabbi's age not to be married but wondered if a wedding in the near future would detract from the mission they were all now embarked on.

The rest of the evening was spent in quiet contemplation. Maryam had left with the rest of the women, undeterred by Simon's outburst, although she was a little afraid of him, she promised she would return. The man was saddened by the attitude of the men to Mara. He understood the culture from which they came but did not share their feelings. He had been brought up to respect women since he lived in Egypt where women were treated as equals. He liked the company of women, they were often a refreshing change. Sometimes they were simple honest souls, others were feisty and challenging, like Salome, one of Mara's friends. She had taken him to one side one day and asked, "Who are you? As a man who comes to stay at my home, eats from my table and sleeps on my couch, when I, a woman, do not know you. Is it seemly? I ask again, Who are you and where do you come from?"

He studied her for a moment before replying, making up his mind what to tell her. Then he said, fixing her with his eyes, "I come from God and what is undivided. To him there is no 'man' or 'woman' so there is no problem with whomever I stay." Being wise Salome understood what he was saying and was content. She became one of his most ardent followers and brought many converts to his cause. Other women provided food and shelter. If their homes were large enough the disciples would meet to pray, they were called house churches. Women seemed to like his charismatic personality. They would join the meetings, bring their children and often go ahead of the group to arrange accommodation for the night. He thought of many of the women he had met. There was Martha, a forthright soul who ruled the roost at her home in Bethany and was a wonderful cook. Her sister, Mary, who was headstrong and occasionally wilful but whose heart was in the right place, whose father indulged her with expensive oils and perfumes, and their brother, Lazarus, a fine young man who would have been one of the twelve had his health been better. Then there was the vivacious Joanna. She was the wife of Chusa, Herod's chief steward who kept him amused with court gossip, or helped their security by informing them of any military activity in the area.

He could read a person's mind and look into their soul when first they met, like the woman by Jacob's well in Samaria where he rested one day. He had asked her to draw him some water as he had no bucket. She had rounded on him calling him an arrogant Jew and she would fetch her husband. He calmly replied that she had no husband, had buried five previous husbands and was not married to the man she now lived with. She was amazed at his knowledge and proclaimed him a prophet, but still sneered at him saying,

"You Jews say we must worship in Jerusalem. Our fathers have always worshipped on this mountain so you say we are not proper Jews." He fixed her with his gaze and replied, "The time is now for people to worship God in spirit and in truth anywhere they choose." The Samaritan woman said, "When the Messiah comes He will tell us everything." Quietly but firmly he had told her,

"The time is now. I am He." Then she was frightened off by the approach of the disciples who had been in the town to buy supplies. She had left her water jar and ran back to the village to tell people what had happened. Many came to meet him and were converted to his mission.

Then he thought about his mother. There was no question that he loved her, but it seemed that whenever they met, which was quite often, she would say or do something that irritated him. She did not approve of his choice of disciples. She questioned what he was doing, worried about his well-being and gave him such sorrowful looks with pain in her eyes that it made his heart sink at times. He knew he was disrespectful at times, calling her 'woman' instead of "mother'. He sighed and vowed to make it up to her somehow, see that she was well looked after.

He cheered up considerably when he thought of Mara, she whom he loved above all women. She was witty, intelligent and a pleasure to be with. His heart leapt whenever he saw her approaching. He could read her thoughts and laughed when she complained, "Is nothing private these days?" That she loved him in return was beyond doubt. They would talk for hours or for just a few snatched minutes as he always seemed to be surrounded by people wanting to hear him, see him, touch him or question him. She understood him and what he was doing and supported him. She too asked him many questions although she had said, "Don't be angry with me if I ask too many because I know I shouldn't question you." He did not mind at all. Later she had said, "I do understand what you are saying, but sometimes I'm afraid. Simon doesn't like me. He glowers at me and sometimes draws his fingers across his throat to threaten me." So he knew of Simon's attitude before his outburst and was saddened by it. Then he prayed to God for help in showing him a way to pacify Simon and make peace between them. Before he slept he thought of Mara's warm touch, the way she threw her head back when she laughed and her sweet lips. He sent her his love and wished her sweet dreams, before sleeping peacefully.

The next morning, after eating bread, cheese and fruit washed down with milk, he reminded them all to keep and teach the laws of Moses but offered a different way of life, one of love to friends, families and enemies alike. This was a new way of looking at the world. God would provide for them, tell them the words to say and keep them safe, like their human father would. John asked what God looked like and he asked in return.

"Do you resemble your father...? Then those who have seen me have seen God." Those who were travelling that day set out with renewed faith and zeal. The master had always emphasized that he was human ["If I am cut, I bleed like anyone else"]. He had also described himself as a fisherman, they saw he was a healer, could perform miracles and was their rabbi, their teacher, even a prophet. How could they not believe in him? He also told them that he was a shepherd who looked after the weak, went looking for those that went astray, nurtured the strong and urged them to do the same. He then added in a strange voice, "A good shepherd is willing to lay down his life to save his flock. Remember my words in times to come. With remembering comes understanding." They promised to do so then went about their work.

His energy seemed boundless, his knowledge endless. He transmitted his enthusiasm to the disciples daily. He taught practical things and how to teach them to their converts in ways the weak, poor, sick and miserable would understand. He transformed their values on how to live in harmony with their neighbours, to be patient – even conquerors come and go, to be open and truthful, to have faith in God even if they have to suffer hardship on earth. Their reward will be joy and a place in the Kingdom of Heaven. He did not give them rules to live by but principles and claimed time after time that he was not changing the law but interpreting it differently.

Many of their questions concerned everyday situations. One man asked, "I married my brother's wife, in accordance with the law, because she gave him no children. So, master, whose wife will she be in heaven?" He replied, "She will be nobody's wife. There is no marriage in heaven, only peace harmony and love amongst all."

Gradually as the disciples learned and understood more, his emphasis changed, imperceptibly at first. Whereas he had always insisted that God was the teacher and healer and must

103

always be invoked, he later changed to 'the father', then 'our father', or 'my father' until eventually he began to say, "I say unto you…" The disciples realized that he was speaking with his own authority, saying his own words thus giving a new perspective to his work. They talked amongst themselves, astonished at this new development.

"If he is speaking as a law maker then he must be on a level with Moses," said one. Another thought he might be one of the other prophets reincarnated. "Many of his principles and ways of living are new," was another comment. "So maybe he is greater than even all the prophets."

"How can that be?" said Matthew disparagingly. "There is only one greater than the prophets and that's God himself!" He thought about what he had just said and his eyes grew wide. Realisation was dawning on them but acceptance of this enormity was difficult and doubts arose in their minds. After a while spent in deep silence, John spoke up. "There is only one way to find out," he said gravely, "and that's to ask him."

The disciples met up with the master on the road to Caesarea Philippi. He appeared to be in deep thought so they waited until they reached a quiet resting place out of the sun and sat with their backs against a rock wall overlooking the River Jordan. No one wanted to be the first to ask the question uppermost in their minds. Reading their thoughts, the master asked them a question.

"Who do the people you meet say I am?"

"Elijah," said one.

"John the Baptist," said another.

"I've heard you called a charlatan," called a third. They all seemed to talk at once. 'Moses', 'Jeremiah', 'A new prophet'. The suggestions came thick and fast. The man held up his hands for silence and looked round at each of them.

"And who do you say I am?" There was an awkward pause before anyone spoke, then Simon raised his eyes and spoke in a clear voice, "I think," he said slowly and deliberately, "I think… You are the one we have been waiting for, the one promised by the prophets. I think… you are the Messiah, the Son of God." He held his breath but did not lower his gaze. The others sat like statues, mesmerized, also with bated breath.

The man's face was solemn, then suddenly it lit up with a huge beaming smile. He wanted to punch the air with joy. Jumping up and grasping Simon in a crushing hug he cried, "Simon, son of Jonah, You are indeed blessed by God. Nobody ever said that to you. You must have been told by God Himself! I was right to call you my rock. From this day you will be known as Peter. Not only will you be the bedrock of my church here on earth but I will give you the keys to the Kingdom of heaven itself!"

The tension in the air evaporated and everyone relaxed but the disciples now felt awkward in his presence. Sensing their apprehension, he said, "Look, I am still the man you know. I'm human remember? Not only the Son of God, But the son of Man as well. Nothing has changed between us." Then he became very serious. "A word of warning, my brothers. Nobody must breathe a word of this to anyone. Not to wives, children, friends, brothers, priests, anyone. Do you understand? People are not ready for this revelation yet. There are things I have to do, things which will upset the powers that be. There are trying times ahead for all of us, especially for me. For now, let us continue with our mission here on earth. We must work harder, longer, further afield. Time is running out and we need thousands more to believe and have faith."

"I don't quite understand the difference between belief and faith," said Andrew. "To me they are the same… aren't they?"

"There is a difference," replied the rabbi, slipping back into teaching mode. "Belief is what you know to be true, faith is what you think is true. You believe that I am human. You have faith in me as the Son of God. Does that answer your question?"

From that day, he taught, led, pushed and drove them almost to the point of exhaustion, even getting angry with them if they missed the point or asked basic questions. "Aren't you listening to me? Don't you hear what I am saying? Don't you yet understand what I am about and what I am doing? I will not be with you forever and you must be ready to do my work, lead my sheep. Bring the lambs safely into the fold. You must bear the burden when I am gone. Everything I am trying to bring about rests on your shoulders. Do not let me down."

He gave them endless advice and information on the law, how they should answer questions about divorce, adultery, wrong doing, how to pray, fasting, paying of taxes, anything which people might ask them. He also taught about how to deal with the priests. "Listen to them, obey the law but don't be like them. They are self-satisfied, glory seekers who only pay lip service to God."

"Then why go to the synagogue?" they asked.

"Because it is the law," he replied. "But you can pray to God anywhere and at any time. The Father is always listening."

One evening, after a particularly long teaching session, one disciple came to him and said, "Lord, there is so much to learn and remember, the laws the commandments, all the new things you have told us. Which of all these is the greatest that we must never forget?"

The master replied, "All the words of the prophets hang on two things. First, 'love your God with all your heart, mind and soul.' Second, 'Love your neighbour as yourself' If you truly live by these standards then nothing can go wrong. Now, eat, rest and sleep. Tomorrow will be another tiring day."

Although physically exhausted, the disciples did not complain. They went about their work with renewed zeal and vigour. Simon, now Peter, pushed himself hard. He was pleased with his new name and his responsibility as the keeper of the Keys. He even managed to control his jealousy of Maryam but avoided her as much as possible. He grudgingly admitted to himself that she worked as hard as any of them, if not harder. She was responsible for finding people to give them food and shelter, or money to buy supplies. Judas was the keeper of the purse, did most of the buying and distributed alms to the poor. Maryam also learned with them the master's wisdom and his skills. No one thought to ask her to leave again. She spent a lot of her time with women and children, telling them stories and encouraging them to believe the Kingdom of God was coming soon.

She tried to spend as much time as she could, alone with Yeshi, which was not easy as he seemed to spend every waking moment working harder and harder. She made sure he ate properly even though he sometimes said he had been fed by God. She merely fixed him with her gaze and said,"EAT." She told him what she had done, seen and heard and begged him that she should do more to lighten his load. He asked her to reassure his mother and keep her well which she agreed to do. She knew of Simon's new name of Peter.

"He is a good man even though he does not approve of me," she sighed. "You have chosen well, he works harder than any of them but he too is human and I think he might let you down if things go badly for you." Yeshi shook his head slowly and whispered, "Don't worry Mara, my love. Everyone stumbles occasionally but they pick themselves up determined to be more careful and not stumble again. I think they will all stumble at some point."

"Not me, Yeshi, Whatever happens," she insisted, "I will be with you to the end and beyond." The memory of her vision once again flashed through her mind. "I know, Mara," he assured her gently holding her face up so he could look into her eyes ."You will be the last and the first to see me."

Not quite sure of his meaning, she sat close to him. As before they talked for as long as they could, holding each other close or resting their heads on the other's lap. Always they parted with an embrace and passed on their private thoughts to one another.

Everyone's hard work paid off. Each disciple attracted many people to the new faith. Simon the zealot and Judas breathed fire into the bellies of the young men who desperately wanted to see the restoration of the Kingdom of Israel. Although some who did not particularly want to listen could not help but hear the message and exhortations of James. John appealed to women and children, with his boyish good looks, open face and winning smile. He did most of the healing with his small, but strong hands. Phillip and Nathanial were successful with the upper echelons of society, being able to speak different languages, teach and persuade with knowledge and confidence. Although targeting the Jewish population, many from other religions were attracted to the idea of monotheism and were converted. Phillip and Nathanial understood that God had created not only Israel but the world and therefore, it was logical that He was the one true God of everyone. They had no problem meeting and talking with gentiles. Matthew and Thomas had most success with the artisans and traders in the towns. James, son of Alpheus and his son Thaddeus went into the villages and fields talking to the poor labourers in the countryside. Andrew and Peter concentrated their efforts along the shores of Galilee and the Mediterranean. They knew the concerns of those in the fishing industry and reassured them, saying that better days were coming if only they will believe and support the new leader.

So successful were they all that people were baptized in their droves. There was an excitement in the air that was almost tangible. Enthusiasm and expectation was high. Hope was restored to them and all were keen to see, hear and touch this new, charismatic man, who they hoped would lead them to a better life in the newly restored, united kingdom of Israel.

CHAPTER TEN

The Miraculous Healer

In the early days the man had thought long and hard about his mission. He would never make the same mistakes he had made in his own home village. He still felt hurt that his own neighbours had come close to stoning him. Had they succeeded, his mission would have been over before it had begun. People were just not ready to accept his words if he just blurted out, "I am the promised one. I am the Son of God!" He had to be much more subtle than that, a much softer approach was needed.

On his journey to Capernaum he mainly talked to fellow travellers, families or small groups. He told stories from the scriptures, gave blessings, carried out baptisms or healed the sick, of whom there were many. Children especially were prone to fevers, disease and sickness. Malnutrition, lack of clean water to drink and poverty all contributed to early deaths of these poor innocents. Crop failure caused by drought brought many families close to starvation. His knowledge of herbs and wild plants found in the hedgerows helped him to make concoctions to clean and heal sores or wounds. He set broken limbs with such skill that the bones seemed to heal overnight.

Everyone knew about ritual cleansing with water but little of personal hygiene, resulting in many skin or internal diseases. "Water," he explained to them, "is the source of life. It cleans not only the body but also purifies the spirit. To go under the water and rise out of it is like being born again." They listened to him and some took his words to heart but others did not. It was either too far from the river to fetch clean water or they did not want to change their ways.

Although impressed by this charismatic man and grateful for his healing, they did not regard him as anything particularly special. There were many others in the country who were healers, like Hanan, a labourer by day, preacher and healer of the sick whenever he could. There were many others who told stories and explained the scriptures, so this new rabbi was just one of many. It was unusual however that one man could do both with such ease and without fuss so he was easily remembered in the days to come. Village gossip about him spread quickly, not only about the healings, but about the blessings and breaking of bread. "It never tasted so good and there was always enough left for the next day. Odd that," they said.

Once he had selected his twelve, the man taught them how to heal. "It is a way into their hearts and minds," he said. "They will wonder how it was possible and then remember that you called upon God to do the healing through you. This way you are restoring their faith as well as their bodies."

They practised on each other and on animals until they were confident enough in their abilities to include healing in their daily work, quickly becoming adept. Andrew and Phillip became particularly skilled in exorcism. Many people believed in demons or evil spirits invading the body and whilst the disciples understood that the cause was usually a mental illness, it was easier to go along with popular belief and order 'Satan' to leave the body.

In the early days they had not always been successful. One day Phillip had attempted and failed to cast out an evil spirit from a young boy who had suffered from convulsions and foaming at the mouth almost from being born. His father brought him to the master and begged him to drive out the demons saying, "If you can do anything to help us, then take pity on us and heal him."

"IF," the master asked incredulously, "IF I can' you ask. Anything is possible if you believe." The man fell on his knees and begged, "Please help me to overcome my unbelief." Seeing a crowd approaching, the master quickly asked God to command the demons to leave the child's body and never return. Immediately the screaming, foaming and shaking ceased and the boy was given back to the father. People who witnessed this healing were amazed at what they had seen.

Later Phillip came to the master and asked why he had failed so miserably. "I did everything you told us and nothing happened," he said, hanging his head. "I am not worthy of you and have let you down." Quietly the master replied, "It was because you did not have enough faith in yourself and in God. You must truly believe that you can do these things. Nothing, I say, nothing, is impossible if you have faith. You could move mountains if your faith is strong enough. Now go and do God's work." All the disciples re-doubled their efforts to hone their skills.

On occasions the one suffering from the demons recognized the healer as the Son of God and called out to leave them alone but he quieted them and cast out the evil spirits so the sufferers were no longer a danger to themselves or those around them. Some had been so violent that they were tied up or no one would come near them. The master felt great compassion for these poor wretches and always gave them hope.

Word of the healings, especially the spectacular ones like casting out evil spirits, quickly spread and more and more people came to be healed or bring their loved ones. As the disciples travelled further and further afield through Galilee, Judea, Phoenicia, Decapolis and across the Jordan into Damascus in Syria where was a large Jewish population, so their numbers of converts grew. From a trickle in the early days, starting with one then twelve then seventy, the steady stream increased to a torrent then a raging flood of thousands of converts filled with hope and belief that Judgement day was coming soon and they would be blessed with a better way of life. Always after preaching or healing the disciples would urge them to be baptized, and believe the kingdom of God was nigh.

It was physically and mentally exhausting for all of the followers but none of them even thought of dropping out or leaving. They were refreshed and fired up by the master's example, enthusiasm, certainty and encouragement. They all had utter faith in him and what they were doing. If healing was the way to people's hearts, then so be it.

Sometimes the crowds came in their thousands, whole families willing to travel long distances to be cured of their ailments and to hear the charismatic rabbi preach. If they gathered on the seashore he would preach from a boat. If they met on a hillside he would climb further up the slope so they could all see and hear him. People waited many hours, patiently, to be healed. Often they would still be there as the evening approached.

On one such occasion, seeing that there were many small children, Andrew asked the master if he should send the children home as it would soon be dark and they would need to eat. Instantly the rabbi turned on him and said, "Leave them alone. They are the children of God and as yet are without sin. Everyone who wants to enter the Kingdom of God should be as innocent as these little ones. Let them keep coming. However," he continued thoughtfully, "some of them have been with us several days. They must by now have eaten all the food they brought with them so they will be hungry. We must feed them."

"Where will we buy so much food in this remote place?" asked Phillip. "Even if Judas has enough money."

"We will share what we have. Go and see what you can find." Andrew came back with a small boy, carrying a reed basket. "This is all I can find," he said. "It isn't much. Just five loaves and two fishes but the boy wants you to have it as thanks for healing his mother."

"It is enough," the master acknowledged. "Tell the people to sit in groups and then feed them," He laid the loaves on a woven tray, gave thanks to God for providing them, broke them into pieces and blessed them. Repeating his actions with the two small fish, he passed the tray to Andrew saying, "Share it with the others and take it to the people. Tell everyone to take what he needs and pass the rest to his neighbour. There will be sufficient."

When everyone had eaten his fill the disciples collected the remains which filled several baskets. All the people marvelled at what they had just seen and a buzz went round the crowd.

"It is a miracle."

"It's a sign."

"He's a prophet."

"This is God's doing."

"He's been sent by God," were the comments they made to each other.

Aware of what was being spread by the crowd and afraid that the murmur would become a clamour and maybe hysteria would break out, he told the disciples to disperse the multitude telling them to go home. He himself slipped quietly away into the evening dusk and went further up the mountain to rest and pray, wondering if this action had been a step too far, too soon.

Unable to find him the disciples collected the uneaten food and returned to Capernaum, where they knew the master would come to them. They gave the food to the beggars and the poor in the town then each went their own way to stay with their families or friends for the night.

James and John went with Peter and Andrew to their boat for the night. They had all missed the rocking of the boat and the slapping of the waves to lull them to sleep and could think of nowhere better. After discussing the events of the strange day when they had been shown even more power of the master, they slept soundly, only to be wakened by a storm buffeting their boat and threatening to capsize them. Huge waves were breaking across the bow, the wind howled and the sails looked as though they would be torn to shreds any minute. The four men, although seasoned sailors and used to the vagaries of the sea, were afraid for their safety and the boat's ability to weather the storm.

They looked across the angry waves and saw an apparition in the darkness and were even more terrified, thinking that a ghost had come to warn them of their doom. A voice called out to them saying,

"Don't be afraid. It is I, the rabbi," Peter called back. "If it is really you, let me come to you without sinking!" Without hesitation the man invited him to come, so Peter climbed out of the boat and into the water. The other three watched, wide eyed and hearts thumping. Peter walked towards the master but he suddenly became aware of the strong wind and ferocious waves. He panicked and began to sink but the master caught him. "You didn't trust me enough!" he shouted above the noise of the wind. "You lost your faith and doubted me. That is why you sank." They both clambered back into the boat and the storm abated. The brothers were awed by what they had witnessed.

"This is truly the Son of God," whispered John. "Even the wind and waves obey Him," Peter said nothing but silently vowed never to doubt ever again, not even for a second.

Healing was tiring work requiring great concentration and effort. Each time the man or disciple cured someone they felt some of their strength leave their bodies and were exhausted by nightfall. One day, the crowds pressed in on them as usual, clamouring for attention, the man felt some of his strength leave him.

"Who touched me?" he asked sharply.

Puzzled Peter said, "Lots of people master. It's a big crowd today. Many are pressing up against you. We cannot protect you completely."

"No," he flashed back. "Someone deliberately touched me with a special purpose. Who was it?" No one owned up. He waited. Eventually a woman came forward, shaking with fear and threw herself down at his feet. She admitted that she had touched the hem of his garment as he passed by.

"Sir," she said, "I am weak from bleeding for many years and I thought that if I could just touch you I would be healed. I am sorry if I have offended you." He raised her to her feet and announced to the people round about,

"This woman has been healed, not by me but by her own faith in God." And to her he said gently, "daughter, go in peace. Your faith has made you whole." He was pleased that his mission was succeeding and that more and more people were having faith in him.

It was not only the poor who came to him for help and advice. Rich men, Sadducees and even court officials who were desperate for help for their family members, usually sons or daughters, called upon him to heal their loved ones. When they saw what he did always with God's help the whole household, including servants were usually were converted.

Although they aimed their work at the Jewish population, many others heard of this band of preachers and came to listen to the master and his disciples' message. When visiting the area near Sidon a Canaanite woman kept following them, begging one of them to come and heal her daughter by casting out her demons. They did not respond to her at first, ignoring her presence and her pleas. Then she called out in a desperate voice

"Lord, son of David, have mercy on me." The disciples urged him to send her away as she was not Jewish. The master turned to her and told her that he was sent to care for the lost children of Israel, but she persisted and knelt in front of him, beseeching him to help her. Goading her further he said "It is not right that I should take the children's bread and feed it to the dogs!"

She quickly retorted, "But even the dogs eat any crumbs they can get that fall from the master's table."

Impressed with her determination and understanding he told her, "Woman, you have great faith in me. Your request is granted. Go, your daughter is healed." The disciples then understood that God's compassion was for all those who believed in Him and did not discriminate between Jew and gentile in their flocks.

Not all Romans were hated by the Jews. Some, although keeping strictly to the laws and orders of the oppressors, loved living in this part of the Roman Empire, especially since the climate was much better than that of Gaul or Britannia. If the locals were treated fairly they did not rebel unnecessarily. One such Roman was the Centurion in charge of the garrison in Capernaum where the disciples had made their base. As long as they did not break the law, he mainly ignored them. The townsfolk did not fear this soldier and he dealt kindly and fairly with them. Many of them found employment at his home or garrison, gardening, cleaning cooking or selling him supplies. Having been at his post many years, the Centurion knew many people from the area and kept abreast of what was going on. He was attracted to the idea of monotheism but although he never converted to Judaism he gave enough money to the people to build a synagogue in the town.

He heard stories of John the Baptist and of the new leader. What was going on in the area was on everyone's lips, so he could not help hearing about the healings and miracles from his family, servants and his soldiers. He was aware of the message about the coming of the kingdom of their god but was not worried. The might of Rome was invincible! He was, however, intrigued by the rabbi. He had seen him once preaching in the market square and thought his words were powerful. They did not speak but their eyes had met, seemingly with recognition of each other's status.

Those who served him were loyal and trusted him. He returned their trust and loyalty, equally, serving their best interests as his own. When a long time servant became ill he provided all the help he could but the man, who had over the years become his much valued friend, did not respond and was near to death. Knowing that the healer was travelling from Capernaum to Bethsaida he sent some of his friends to ask him to come and heal the servant. He realised that it was frowned upon to enter the house of a non-Jew and even more so that of a Roman, therefore he himself waited at the gate of his house. As the healer approached he called out, "Lord, you don't have to come inside. I am not worthy of you, not even to ask this favour of you. I myself am a man of authority and if I give an order I know that it will be carried out without question. You also have that same authority, so just say the word and we both know that my faithful servant will be cured."

The man was taken aback by the Centurion's words and turned to those following him. "Nowhere in the kingdom of Israel have I found such great faith in me," he declared.

The Centurion gave the healer his thanks, knowing that his servant would now have recovered. "If there is anything I can ever do for you in return…" he started to say, but the man cut him off. Fixing him with a stare he said,

"If ever there is… You will know," then turning on his heel he continued on his way to Bethsaida with a spring in his step.

Although healing was part of the mission, the man did not want it to be the main element. It certainly attracted attention and drew the crowds but he did not want people to come just for healing or spectacle. Some who came to him asked for a sign before believing his words.

"Show us a miracle," they almost demanded. "Then we will believe," at which he grew angry and refused.

There were other healers at the same time, so minor cures did not matter too much but the more spectacular almost miraculous healings caused much interest and speculation impelling him to tell each individual to say nothing about him. This was almost impossible when he cured the blind, the mute or those who could not walk. In order to be re-admitted to the congregation of the synagogue, the one cured had to go to the priest to be ritually purified and to make a sacrifice. Inevitably this led to questions such as,

"How was it done?"

"Who did this?" and

"When was this done?"

The answers troubled the priests. They were disturbed by all the tales going round about this healer, his following and his message, so they were determined to keep their eyes and ears open for any small thing which broke the Laws of Moses.

Not all the priests were against him. There were those who listened and admired his knowledge of the scriptures and the way he explained their meanings. Others admired his power and believed his message came from the God of Moses and Abraham. One such priest was Jairus, ruler of a synagogue. He had heard of the healing power of God through this man and was desperate for him to come and heal his daughter. When he saw the rabbi nearby he threw himself at his feet, begging piteously for him to come to his home.

"My only daughter is dying and I cannot imagine life without her," he sobbed. "She is the light of my life and is totally without sin. Please, I beg you, hurry!" The master was more than willing to do as he was asked. It was unusual for a man to openly show such affection for a daughter. He was also impressed that the priest believed he could cure her.

However, as they hurried towards the house, a close friend of Jairus ran up to him and putting his hands on his shoulder quietly said, "My friend, it is too late. Your daughter is dead. I'm sorry. There is no need to bring the healer anymore."

Jairus almost fell down with grief but the healer steadied him saying, "It is not too late. Do not fear, just believe. Your daughter is not dead, she is sleeping." Before even arriving at the house they heard the ululation of grief, wailing and sobbing. He silenced them with a raised hand telling them that the girl was simply sleeping and not dead but they shook their heads and did not believe him having seen her body for themselves.

Taking the parents, Peter, Andrew, James and John with him he entered the room where the girl lay. He took her small, cold hands in his and gently raised her up to a sitting position, murmuring

"My child, Get up!" the colour returned to her cheeks, her eyelids fluttered open and she stood up, much to the astonishment and joy of her parents. "Get her something to drink," he told her mother, "and do not tell anyone what you have just witnessed. I said she was sleeping. Remember?" Jairus thanked him profusely and wanted them all to stay for a while but anxious not to have to answer questions, he replied that they had to be on their way. They left with money and enough food for their travels, promising to return one day. On their journey they discussed this new development in the master's healing ability. He told them that what they had just been privy to was strictly between them and not to broadcast it to anyone.

"It is not yet time to reveal such actions," he warned them. "The people are not yet ready and the powers that be will try to discredit me. Just remember, it is the power of the Father working through me." The four brothers gave their solemn promise and felt closer to him than ever before.

Because he was so well versed in the law and scriptures, he was often invited to the home of a Pharisee for a meal along with other guests of lawyers, priests and wealthy business men to discuss topics of the day. Some of these people were receptive to his teachings, like Nicodemus who had been born again by being baptized, whilst still maintaining their Judaism. Others were openly hostile and often challenged him, or waited until they perceived he had made an error to mock or criticize him. He always answered his critics, usually with a question of his own to make them think.

On one such occasion, eating at the house of his friend Nicodemus, he noticed a man with a withered hand. He felt eyes upon him and knowing what was in their minds asked,

"Who among you would not rescue his son if he fell down a well on the Sabbath?" When nobody answered he rose from his seat, went up to the man and held his hand, quietly invoking God's help. Some of the guests felt uncomfortable.

"He could have waited another day," they muttered, but he rebuked them.

"Is it lawful to do God's work on the Sabbath? Circumcision for example. Healing is God's work, therefore is lawful!" Those listening had no answer. The man calmly went back to his place at the table and resumed eating as though nothing had happened but well aware of the uneasy atmosphere. Nicodemus was impressed by the way his friend had conducted himself.

Whenever he was in Judea, the master stayed at the house of his friend Lazarus, whom he loved like a brother. Lazarus lived in a village called Bethany, less than two miles from Jerusalem across the Kidron Valley. It was a peaceful place where the air was fine and clear. Healthy fig and olive trees gave shade from the searing sun, vines grew in neat lines across the hillside, goats grazed the sparse grass and the birdsong at dawn and dusk filled the air with music.

Lazarus' father was a rich merchant, trading in spices and expensive oils to make perfume, which his youngest daughter, Mary applied liberally. His other daughter, Martha, was a formidable woman who ruled the roost, especially the kitchen, with a rod of iron. She was the best cook he had ever known. Her pieces of meat, threaded on wet sticks and roasted over the fire set in the outside wall of her kitchen, were the tenderest, juiciest ever and her sweetmeats, layers of pastry filled with dried grapes, baked to perfection in her clay oven, then soaked in honey from her own hives, were to die for.

All the disciples had stayed there at some time, eating her out of house and home. She grumbled and scolded them endlessly, but secretly she loved them all and their company.

One spring morning, as the disciples gathered together on the banks of the River Jordan, a young man came striding through the crowd, dusty and grimy as though he had travelled long and far.

"Sir," he said, making straight for the master, "I have brought a message from the sisters, Martha and Mary, in

Bethany. Their brother, Lazarus, is very sick and they ask that you come to him. I have already spent two days travelling to find you and I fear that by the time you get there it will be too late."

The master thanked him for coming, assured him that all would be well and told him to rest. He then took himself a little way apart from the others to pray. There were still two more weeks to Passover when he knew that his mission would be at an end. The time was right for the final push. Maybe this would be his final act of healing and he knew that it had to be impressive, quite spectacular, so he prayed fervently for help and determination to do what had to be done. Once successfully completed, there would be no turning back. Then he slept.

The disciples thought it strange that the master did not want to set out immediately to go to his friend but they did not wake him. It was not until the next morning that they set out on their two day journey to Bethany. He was unusually quiet on the way, deep in thought, and did not seem in any hurry to get to their destination. On the morning of the third day they finally reached the outskirts of the village. There were many people around, beginning to gather at the homes of friends and families for the Passover celebrations.

"You're too late," called out a man who recognized them "He was buried four days ago." Martha came out of her house at that moment and walked to meet them, her eyes red with weeping and he usual smiling face darkened with sorrow.

"Why didn't you come earlier?" she wailed. "You could have saved him. If you had been here he would not have died." The master put his arms round her and she sobbed on his shoulder.

"Your brother will rise again," he promised her.

"We will all rise again on resurrection day. I want him back now."

Quietly into her ear he whispered, "I am the resurrection Martha. He who believes in me will never die. Now go and fetch Mary then together we will go and get Lazarus." She looked into his face and nodded imperceptibly.

The master, the sisters, the disciples and many village people walked the path to the burial site outside the village on the hillside. They came upon the cave tomb where Lazarus had lain for four days. A huge circular stone slab covered the cave entrance which took three strong men with stout poles to lever away. As the stone was rolled back and secured with stones so that it would not move, a wave of fetid air swept out of the tomb. The stench of death and decay was almost unbearable causing many to cover their mouth and nose or turn away, coughing.

Deeply moved, with tears trickling down his cheeks, the master stood at the entrance of the tomb. He stretched out his arms, clenched his fists and drew them into his body. He stood so still he seemed to be made of stone, concentration etched on every part of his face. Then he called out in a loud voice so that all those outside could hear him,

"Father, hear me one more time. Help me!" In an even more commanding voice he gave the order to Lazarus to come out of the cave, then fell on his knees and held out his arms.

There was a long drawn out silence as everyone watched and waited with bated breath. Even the birds and the wind were stilled. Eventually they caught sight of a hand, skeleton thin with greying flesh hanging from it, followed by an arm, still wrapped in the binding cloths from his burial, reaching out to take the hands of the healer.

Gasps came from the mouths of all those outside. Some covered their faces because they were afraid, others fell on their knees and wept tears of wonderment. Even the disciples were amazed. They had seen many healings before but none as stunning as this truly miraculous event. Martha and Mary remained standing as joy and happiness radiated from them.

As Lazarus slowly emerged from the tomb, the binding cloths fell away from his body, the flesh filled out on his bones and he was whole again. The healer draped his own cloak round Lazarus' shoulders and slowly and gently led him down the hillside to his home.

The crowd, now recovered from their shock at seeing a dead man brought back to life, cheered and praised the healer saying he was the one sent by God and believed in him. They returned to their homes in Bethany and Jerusalem excitedly spreading the news of the miracle to everyone they met. Never had such a thing happened before. Not even Moses had performed such a wondrous deed.

At Martha's house Lazarus rested, overwhelmed by what had happened. Martha bustled around in the kitchen which she had neglected this last week, preparing a meal for them all. The disciples' conversation buzzed about the after-effects of this raising of the dead.

"It will bring in many more converts," said Matthew.

"Maybe now is the time for an uprising in Jerusalem," added Judas.

"More likely it will upset the Pharisees and cause trouble for us," muttered Thomas.

"Everything will end in Jerusalem for me," sighed the master.

"Then don't go there," said Peter, shrugging his shoulders. "It's simple. Stay away from the Passover week and no harm will come to you!" The master jumped to his feet, anger flashing from his eyes.

"Get thee behind me Satan!" he roared. "Do not tempt me anymore. Everything I have planned and done has been leading up to this. Haven't you been listening to me? This is my destiny. Resurrecting Lazarus is the spark which lights the fire.

I cannot stop now!" Amazed at his outburst the disciples were quieted.

Peter slipped outside and wept. 'I always do and say the wrong thing', he thought, 'how can he call me his rock when I let him down so often?'

Inside, the subdued disciples ate their meal in silence. At the end Mary came in carrying a jar of pure spikenard, an extremely expensive perfume oil. She knelt in front of the master and, much to everyone's amazement poured the whole precious lot over his feet. She then took the scarf from her head and shook out her long dark hair. Gently she wiped the oil from his skin using her locks. The man smiled at her, pleased, even though it was an unnecessary gesture on her part.

Judas grumbled about the expensive waste. "The money that 'nard cost, could have been used to feed the poor," he chuntered.

"Leave her alone," the man ordered. "This anointing is intended as a symbol of respect. She was keeping it for use at my burial, so it was not 'wasted' on me. You will always have poor people round you. But me… I will not be with you much longer. As I have said, my destiny lies in Jerusalem."

Exhausted by the events of the day, he rested on the couch, covered by a thin, woven blanket. He had not been with Mara for a week but knew she was coming to Bethany for Passover. His thoughts told her how much he missed her love and strength to advise console and comfort him. She in turn both warmed and soothed him with her thoughts, so that, at last, he slipped into a dreamless 'nothingness' and rested peacefully.

CHAPTER ELEVEN

Friends And Foes

For two days after the raising of Lazarus the master rested. He was surrounded by friends, disciples and well-wishers. His own family had arrived from Nazareth and he had long been reconciled with his mother and brothers. James and Jude had been baptized and had become ardent believers. Joseph still resisted but no longer was he resentful. He told James that his place should be in Jerusalem to carry on with his work there, even though it could be dangerous in the early days.

He spoke to each of the disciples in turn, reassuring them, answering their many questions and advising them how each could best use his skills and continue in his work. Although they did not like it, each knew that the climax was coming and that their beloved rabbi, master, Lord and friend would no longer be with them. He reminded them of the Prophesy of Jachariah which foretold that the shepherd would be taken from them and the sheep scattered. It would be their mission to gather the sheep and care for them. He repeatedly told them to remember all that he had taught them as in a little while they would understand everything.

He sat with Phillip and Nathanial, eating outside in the garden and urged them as linguists and travellers to write as much as they could recall. "No one knows when the Kingdom of God is coming," he explained. "I am merely the forerunner who is preparing the way. You must tell the truth and people will know how everything has come about." They promised that they would do so, and then Phillip quietly remarked,

"You were anointed with oil by Mary. In Greek the word for anointing is Chrisma and the one anointed is called Christas, so, for us and for all time, you will be known as 'The Christ'." The man hugged them both with tears in his eyes and left them to finish their meal.

He spoke often with Judas, who seemed so excited to be going into Jerusalem at last. The time was ripe, thousands of believers would be there and would heed the rallying call. He firmly believed that the master was the son of their God, the long promised and awaited messiah, King of the Jews, so he was surprised when his lord laughed at him.

"You still don't understand, do you Judas? I am not the son of just our God but the son of the one TRUE God. He was the creator and therefore the God of everyone." Judas could not look him in the face and said, "I am not worthy to even speak His name."

The master took Judas to a spot high up the hillside. "I am going to show you the Kingdom of heaven," he promised. He showed Judas the sky filled with light and angels and told him of the creation of the universe by God.

Judas remembered a dream he had. "I left my Brothers and went to a house filled with important people. Does this mean I will enter the Kingdom of heaven?"

The master replied sadly, "I am showing you the Kingdom now because you will never enter it. Another will take your place." Then he pointed upwards where the stars were just beginning to show in the evening dusk. "One of them holds your destiny, Judas. You are the one whose fate it is to sacrifice this body of mine. That is your destiny. It cannot be changed or denied."

"How can this be, master?" Judas asked sorrowfully. "No one has worked harder than me to bring in converts, to spread the word of God."

"Yes," he answered. "But your hope for the Kingdom is an earthly one. Whereas mine is for one where God rules the hearts and minds of men. That is the difference between us."

"Then it is you who have betrayed us!" Judas cried loudly. "How can I have been so wrong about you?"

"You are not wrong about me," the master shot back sharply. "Everything I have said is true but sometimes you chose to misinterpret or ignore what I said."

"When did I ever ignore you?" the now angry disciple shouted. He stepped closer, until their bodies were nearly touching.

The master, now raising his own voice, replied, "Remember the story about loving your neighbour as yourself? The Good Samaritan? You laughed and asked 'What, even the Romans?' then rolled your eyes as if to say 'This must be a joke!' Even now Judas, I believe that the words coming from your mouth are not coming from you but from the devil himself, just as I was tempted by Satan." Turning away from Judas he ordered in a calmer voice, "Say nothing of this conversation to anyone. Just go and do what must be done." Then he returned to the house and found comfort in the company of Mara.

Judas wept, tears of sorrow, frustration, self-pity then of anger. "Years of my life have been wasted, on what? a dream? I should seek advice straight away." He brushed away his tears and strode off down the hillside to Jerusalem where he sought out the High Priest Caiaphas.

Caiaphas, High Priest, ruler of the Temple in Jerusalem, son-in-law of Annas the former High Priest, was appointed by the Roman governor for his ability to maintain the status quo. Highly respected and feared by the populace, he was the only one allowed entrance into the Holy of Holies to touch the Ark of the Covenant and to speak personally to God. He was extremely rich and powerful, wearing magnificent robes which were beautifully embroidered, adorned with many jewels and carried a gold mitre when he went to the temple each morning and evening to make sacrifice. He commanded a large troop of soldiers to guard the temple and himself. Caiaphas' palatial home was sumptuously decorated with mosaics and fine tapestries, rugs and splendid furniture, fine pottery and bronze jugs. Like the Romans he had underfloor heating and elaborate bathrooms.

As High Priest, Caiaphas presided over the Sanhedrin, the Supreme Court, also situated in the Temple grounds. It was here that the Pharisees, priests, scribes, lawyers gathered to discuss points of law and mete out justice to wrong-doers. Minor crimes were dealt with by local elders or priests. Only the Sanhedrin could sanction penalties for major crimes, such as adultery, murder, abduction, incest and crimes breaking the laws of the Sabbath, of which there were many. Caiaphas adjudicated in many disputes and could deliver the death penalty by stoning to a criminal convicted of a very serious crime. Before any conviction, however, there had to be a witness to the crime who should have warned the malfeasant beforehand. Failure to issue a warning meant the witness would share the guilt.

All the members of the Sanhedrin had heard rumours of this new leader from Galilee. People were calling him a prophet, greater than Moses himself. Some had actually heard him preach and were converted and baptised but kept it secret because of their position in the Sanhedrin. Caiaphas was more concerned for his own position and welfare. Numbers in the synagogues round the country were falling, as was the revenue.

The coffers were running low and fewer people were making sacrifice. Only thoughts of the thousands coming to Jerusalem for the Passover celebrations gave him hope of reversing the trend.

He, too, had heard of this leader, of his teaching, healing and raising people's hopes of a new kingdom. He sent out watchers and listeners to report to him personally everything they saw or heard and was perturbed by their findings. He and Annas discussed the topic frequently, becoming more and more alarmed.

"Something has to be done about him," stated Annas, who was also afraid for their position and authority. "We are responsible to the Governor for keeping the peace. If this madman stirs up trouble in Jerusalem at Passover, there may be riots that we cannot control."

Caiaphas agreed with his father-in-law. "If there is a mass riot here there will be much blood shed by the Romans and then retribution throughout the whole of the land. I will be ousted and replaced. I cannot allow that to happen. I have heard that he actually brought a dead man back to life. Whether this is true or not I cannot say but the very rumour itself is enough to make many more people turn to this upstart. Nothing good ever came out of Galilee. We must get rid of him. Better one man dies than a whole nation. The problem is, 'how' 'where' and 'when'. It must be water-tight and legal. Any slip-ups will spark off an insurgency, and that will not be tolerated. I have to find a way of knowing his movements and I pray it will be outside Jerusalem, in a quiet spot. The fewer who know about this, the better."

The answer to Caiaphas' prayer came the next evening in the form of Judas, of whom he was, at first very suspicious.

"You are one of his inner circle, a disciple, are you not? How can I trust what you say?" he queried.

Judas replied, "Because he misled me – all of us. When he spoke of the coming of the Kingdom of God to re-unite all Israel, we all thought, at least Simon and I thought, he meant throwing out the Romans. I was ready to give my life to this end and die a free man, as are thousands of others. Instead of a vengeful God, he only advocates 'love' and 'peace'. Love thy neighbour? The Romans? Never! I feel cheated and angry. He must be stopped, so that when the Messiah, the true deliverer comes, we will be ready."

Caiaphas' spirit soared. Here in front of him was the instrument with which he would strike down this usurper whom threatened his whole way of life.

"My son," he purred, "I truly feel your pain, hurt and disappointment. This man has used you and then betrayed you. But what can I do? He has done nothing wrong in Jerusalem and we don't know where he is to question him. We would like to talk to him and I'm sure the other members of the Sanhedrin would welcome the chance to hear him explain himself. How can we find him though, that is the problem."

"Easily," answered Judas. "I am with him most of the time. When the time is right, be it day or night, I will come to you, so be prepared at all times."

"Thank you, my son," murmured Caiaphas ingratiatingly. "I will be ready and welcome the opportunity to meet him. Now go with my blessing… and a little something for your trouble… until we meet again." Caiaphas pressed a small leather bag into Judas' hand and showed him to the door. When Judas had gone, the sanctimonious expression on his face slipped away and a look of sadistic joy and anticipation took its place. He could hardly wait to tell Annas of his unexpected success.

After supper, the man sat apart with Mara, her head on his shoulder. He related what had transpired between himself and Judas.

"I felt the heat of anger and sorrow between you," she sighed. "I wish it didn't have to be this way. I know you say it is your destiny to be betrayed and die, but isn't it enough that people love you, follow you and have God in their hearts? I would like us to leave, right now, run away back to Egypt and live like a family. I must tell you that I am with child. Doesn't that change everything? How am I to live if you are dead?"

He hugged her closer and kissed her tenderly, forehead, eyes, cheeks and lips. "Mara," he laughed delightedly, "this is wonderful news. If there was any other way I would take it but I am who I am and must fulfil the Prophesies. The wheels are set in motion and cannot be stopped. I give you my heart and my love; my body will be taken by the Romans and my soul belongs to God. I must be crucified and rise again after three days. This way and only this way will people believe in all that I have said and done. Mara, my angel, you have taught me so many things. I do have a human body and heart. Our love is as pure as our love for God and His for us. Ours is a holy matrimony, our ecstasy is akin to the intense love I feel for my father. I am filled with passion when I talk to Him and He talks to me. Don't be afraid for the future, I will watch over you, see you come to no harm. When your time comes you will bear a daughter. Call her Sophia, for she was the wise one who once communed with the Creator, bringing beauty into the world. We may not be able to speak privately together again. Things will happen quickly from now on. Know that I love you deeply and will be with you throughout all eternity." He gently lifted her to her feet and held her close for a long time. Then he kissed her farewell with a deep passion and yet with sorrow in his eyes. Releasing her he turned resolutely and strode off to where the disciples were seated round the fire-pit. Only Peter gave her a menacing glare as she sank back to the ground and wept softly.

"I'm looking forward to this week," remarked John. "If things go according to plan it should be exciting. We haven't been into Jerusalem for a long time."

"It will be different," the master nodded, settling himself down between Peter and John. "I've always said 'be careful – don't make waves and rock the boat' but this time many people will recognise us, know what we have done or will want to meet us. It will be an interesting time but then for me it will be over and you will be on your own."

"We won't let anything happen to you, master," Peter chipped in. "We'll all stick to you no matter what."

The man tilted his head back and snorted ,"You Peter," he chortled, "I don't think so. You will be so scared you won't even admit to knowing me!"

"Never," promised the fisherman unbelievingly. "I may have let you down in the past but never again."

The man shrugged his shoulders. "It is true," he said lowering his voice, "you will deny you have ever seen or met me."

Peter stared in shock. "How can you say such things!" he demanded. "I love you, we all do, like a brother."

"And I you," the master agreed. "But I know you Peter. Once the shepherd has gone, the flock will scatter. When you come back together you will all be stronger than ever, Mark my words and remember."

"Nonsense," huffed Peter, rising to walk off his irritation.

"What of me Lord?" enquired John thoughtfully. "What do you want me to do? To be honest, I'm scared. I know what will happen to you but what do you want of me?"

"It's alright to be scared, John. We are only human. Fear sometimes weakens us but at other times we become stronger. My fear is that I won't be strong enough to see this through to the end. When I think of the pain that I must suffer and that which I will cause others, I just want to hide, but we have come too far to stop now. So, stay with me John, you who I can rely on most, you who loves me so much you will see me through this week even if I waver. When I am gone, though, I want you to promise me that you will take care of my mother. She did not ask for any of this and will grieve that her eldest son has been taken from her."

John promised but asked, "Where shall I take her, master? Where will be safe for both of us?" A memory flashed through the man's mind and he smiled.

"I know the perfect spot," he recalled. "There is a pretty place on the side of a hill overlooking the port of Ephesus. It has a spring of water so pure that it sparkles like the sun and stars together. Take her there. Joseph of Arimathea sails there often and he knows this place. It was he who took me there when I was a boy. It will be a safe place for the rest of her life. She deserves peace and tranquillity after what I have made her suffer." The two men clasped each other to seal the bargain and the master felt his cheek wet with the tears of his best loved disciple.

By now it was well and truly night. The dark velvety sky showed a myriad of sparkling stars and a quarter moon. No clouds spoiled the sight or wind disturbed the trees. Even the birds and animals had settled to their slumbers. Only the subdued chatter of those left in the garden carried on the air. Martha came to her door way and grumbled,

"I know you haven't got homes to go to. You're welcome here, but, for goodness sake Shut up and get some sleep and let me get mine. I've got a busy day tomorrow, an early start in the morning and so have you if you are going into the city." Where upon she closed the heavy wooden door and lowered the latch.

In the city, Caiaphas snored contentedly. He had consumed a copious amount of wine and was happy in the certain knowledge that his position as High Priest was secure.

He looked forward to re-appointment for a further term of office.

Peter slept fitfully, still upset by the accusation of denial by the master. He vowed it would not happen, that he would be strong and watchful.

John lay for a long time thinking about his new responsibilities. He would stay close to the master and encourage him when necessary. Then he thought of Mary and his own mother in Bethsaida. He hoped she would understand him leaving her and his country behind but he knew there were other brothers, friends, neighbours and of course Zebadee her husband to care for her.

Judas had positioned himself away from the others. It was cold and he wrapped his garments tightly round himself as he lay on the ground. He did not know if he dreamed or had a vision but he saw himself with Caiaphas in a courtroom. The faces of the men in the Sanhedrin changed to those of the disciples and many of the other followers. They were no longer in the senate but in a stony field instead, where nothing grew. He could see their angry faces in front of him but could not hear what they were shouting. Suddenly they picked up stones and were hurling them at him, cutting and bruising him until he fell. He tried to protect himself but could not. Everything went dark and the ground was shaking. He opened his eyes to see Simon standing over him roughly shaking his shoulder.

"Shut up man!" Simon fumed. "You were having a nightmare, shouting and waking everybody up! Have some water and then rest."

Mara lay curled up on her cot inside the house, covered by a fine blanket which Martha herself had woven with an intricate pattern. She found it hard to sleep and thought about the living thing inside her. She gently caressed where it lay in utter peace and tranquillity.

"He has given you to me. It is such a pity he will not be there to watch you grow up," she whispered under her breath. "It will be a hard life, little one, but I will look after you for both of us." She thought she had no more tears to shed but felt one more trickle down her cheek and wet the cushion beneath her head and was filled with self-pity. "Why are you doing this to me Yeshi? Don't you love me enough to stay? Don't you want happiness in your life too?" She sent him her thoughts but he did not respond.

After a while, as she tossed and turned in the darkness, she calmed and thought about her life so far. Born a refugee in Egypt, she returned 'home' to a foreign land. She grew up in a man's world, determined to be as good as, if not better, than any of them in everything she did. Being strong willed and sometimes headstrong she succeeded in building up her business and was highly respected but there was something missing in her life – until Yeshi. He accepted her for what she was, respected her not just as a woman but as a person, an equal. Furthermore, he had fallen in love with her as much as she had with him, something she never imagined possible. Best of all, he had cured her demons. She had not had a single attack since that day in the cave deep in the wilderness all those many months ago. He had shared his life with her, his thoughts, doubts, teaching, hopes, fears, his food and yes, even his bed.

She did not regret one minute she had spent with him. She took in a shuddering breath and let out a deep sigh. Now realising that by being selfish, she was letting him down.

"Just like Peter and Judas," she thought in horror. "I can't do this to him. I will show him my love through my strength and support for what he must suffer for my sake as well as everybody else's."

She patted her belly, still taut and flat. "Listen little girl," she whispered. "We are in this together. We will give each other strength and meaning. One day, Sophia, I will tell you about your abba. You have the most wonderful daddy in the whole, wide world." She smiled and she sent her thoughts to him.

"I am so sorry, my love," she apologised, "I am letting you down when you need me most. I won't permit it happen again, I promise on my life. I pray you will forgive me. I will be with you to the end and beyond. Our daughter will grow up to love her abba as much as I do and she will carry on our work, wherever we may be. Be strong, my love. My thoughts are with you always and into life everlasting. So be it." At last she slept and her face relaxed into a contented smile as she dreamed of nothingness.

Outside, the man agonised. His thoughts would not stop cramming into his head and he was filled with self-doubt.

"Am I doing the right thing? Will I be strong enough? Will I be spared at the last minute? What can go wrong? What have I missed or forgotten? What will it feel like to have nails driven into my body?" He reached forward and stirred the embers to get some warmth into his body but still felt chilled to the bone. Shaking his head, he stood up and threaded his way through the sleeping, snoring bodies of his disciples who had been with him for so long.

"And what of you my friends?" he asked himself. "Will you be strong enough to help me? Will you be with me all the way to the end?" He turned his face to the sky and prayed. "Father, they are human, just like me. They are good men and have faith in me and in what You sent me to do. Look after them and guide them because they will be lost for a while without me. Give them strength to do what is right, in Your name and let them continue to do our work after I am gone. I'm so tired abba. Don't let my strength fail me now that I am so close. If I am weak, reassure me. If I falter, steady me. If I fall, pick me up and put me on the right path again. When this is over I will rejoice with you and the Holy Spirit but until then, let your will be my will and together we will succeed. Amen."

At last his thoughts calmed and his mind cleared. He sat cross-legged and prepared to meditate but heard Mara's voice speaking to him. Not as she had done earlier, in anger and self-pity which he had chosen to ignore but with love and affection. He heard her tell their baby that he was her abba, which made him smile and feel proud.

"I hear you my love," he sent back. "I am proud of you. I never doubted you for one minute. You were chosen for me by God and my happiest moments on earth were those spent with you. Remember, you are the last and the first in my life." Contentedly the master returned to his meditation and was refreshed.

THE PASSION

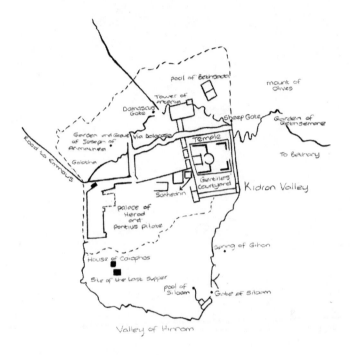

Jerusalem at the time of Christ

CHAPTER TWELVE

Jerusalem

As he approached Bethphage, a small hamlet near Bethany, with several of his disciples, the master sent two of them to Lazarus' field where they would find a donkey and her colt tethered to a gate.

"Why would you want a donkey?" asked Phillip. "We can easily walk the rest of the way."

"Because it fulfils another prophesy, which said 'My people, Israel, look upon your King who comes humbly before you, riding on a donkey.' We will wait here until you return," replied the master settling himself on the ground, resting his back against a boulder and patting the dust from his sandals.

Andrew looked aghast. "We can't just steal it. What if someone asks what we're doing?"

The man laughed. "You will not be stealing it. It is meant to be, but if anyone does ask, just tell them that the master has need of it and there won't be any argument. Now be off with you. Time is getting short."

As they waited at the side of the road for Andrew to return, many people passed them by on their way to Jerusalem. Recognising him as the one who preached, healed the sickness of someone in the family or who had broken bread with them, they called out their greetings or stopped to chat or simply waved.

"Will we see you in Jerusalem?" one asked.

"Come and stay with us and meet our family," said another.

"Do you have enough food?"

"Call on us when you are next in our village," invited several others. Everyone was in high spirits for the holiday and in party mood.

Across the Kidron Valley they could see the city spreading up the hillside, from the groves of olive trees of Gethsemane, to the skyline which was dominated by the Temple building, rising above the city walls. A wisp of black smoke rose into the air, whirling like a demon until it was dispersed by the wind. Smoke, from the burning of sacrificial lambs, doves or goats, and the stench of burning flesh, fur and feathers would be filling the Temple, no matter how many spices and sweet oils were used to cover the smell. There would be a steady stream of worshippers going through the ritual purification baths and many coins going into the Temple coffers.

The Temple itself covered several acres and employed many people. Gentiles were not allowed into the Temple buildings but many gathered in the courtyard or on the Temple steps to sell their wares. The master was saddened to think this had become a centre of commerce instead of the centre of the Jewish faith.

Putting aside these thoughts, the master determined to enjoy his moment. Today was his. It would be the culmination of everything he had worked for. Word of his coming had already reached the city and many people waited by the Damascus Gate to welcome him. For a short time anyway, Jerusalem would belong to him.

All of them had bathed, put on clean, fresh clothes and had trimmed their hair and beards in preparation for their triumphal entry into Jerusalem. Andrew and Matthew arrived back at their resting place leading a donkey with a plaited rope around its neck. Nathanial took off his cloak, folded it and laid it over the donkey's back to make riding more comfortable. The group of disciples, Lazarus' family, his own mother and brothers and Maryam set off on the walk to Jerusalem, less than an hour away. They joined the steady stream of other travellers snaking its way down the road to the city.

As they approached the Damascus Gate, children ran ahead shouting, "He's coming, He's coming." Sounds of a drum beat met their ears, followed by the music of reed pipes and cymbals, mingling with the sounds of excited chatter and laughter. Through the Gate the disciples cleared a path, so he could be seen.

The sight which greeted him surprised even the master. Not only were the crowds lining the streets but they were on every stairway and rooftop and hanging out of the windows. Babies were held out to be touched by him, children were hoisted on their father's shoulders to get a better view. Musicians played and danced before him. Women beat their breasts crying tears of joy and ululating. Men punched the air and shouted their praise. Branches were stripped from palm trees and strewn before him. Children laughed and cheered, throwing flower petals over him as he passed by.

James, in his most thunderous voice shouted, "He's here. This is the one you've been waiting for!"

John took up the rallying cry. "He's the one that Moses promised."

Peter called out ."He's from the line of King David, Praise him."

Nathanial raised his arms in the air, waving, "He's the one who raised Lazarus from the dead."

Phillip cried, "He's the anointed one – the Christ – praise him."

Simon shouted, "Blessed is the King of Israel. Rejoice."

The crowd took up the cry of, "Praise him."

"Hosanna,

"Blessed is the King who comes from God."

The cry of 'Hosanna' became a chant in unison, rising into the air, increasing in volume until it could be heard right across the city and even in the Temple itself.

"What is going on out there?" called Caiaphas to one of the Levites. He was a priest who had come from Tiberius to supplement the Temple officials at this the busiest time of the year. He hurried away to find the cause of the commotion.

When he came back he had a worried frown on his face. "It is the man from Nazareth in Galilee," he reported. "All his followers are with him, saying he is the one that Moses promised would come to be the King of the Jews. The crowds are bowing down and are virtually worshipping him as coming from God."

Caiaphas went white and he gripped his gold mitre for support. Then his face darkened with rage. "This must be stopped," he ranted. "It cannot be allowed to continue. Send word quickly to the Roman garrison and tell them there is an uprising in the city. If it is not stopped immediately a riot will break out and the city may burn. Go and tell them to send out their soldiers."

The priest left the Temple, crossed the gentiles courtyard and into the Roman fortress where he found a centurion. It was the Centurion from Capernaum who, like himself, had been ordered into Jerusalem to swell the number of soldiers at Passover week. It was not his responsibility to quell riots in the streets, others were better trained and more experienced than he. It was his duty to protect the fortress, watch over any prisoners and be adviser to the Governor. He did, however, pass on the message to the duty officer of the day and then climbed to the top of the tower at one corner of the fortress to watch the proceedings.

The soldiers marched out in formation, their breastplates glistening in the sunshine. They were formidable and many people scurried off the streets as they advanced. They formed a barrier, shields touching, across the Via Dolorosa, so named because this was the route taken by prisoners on their way to crucifixion. They waited menacingly, swords at the ready, whilst their leader approached the procession.

The dancing, cheering throng quieted instantly, waiting to see what would happen. Many picked up the cobbles from the street and hid them under their cloaks.

The commander of the riot squad strode up to the man on the donkey. "We don't want any trouble here," he pronounced. "Tell all these people to disperse. I don't want to arrest you since that may spark them off. If there is a riot there will be bloodshed, killings maybe, arrests certainly and crucifixions to follow as a warning to others. The blame will be on your head. We dealt with a skirmish a couple of days ago and the leader, Barabbas, is in custody awaiting sentence. I tell you this so you will be aware of the consequences should you choose to continue this procession. On a signal from me, my men will charge the crowd. Women and children will be hurt." He paused, then, "Well man, what is your answer?"

The disciples listened to the soldier's words and waited for their master's response. Judas was ready for a fight. His hand went to his dagger in his belt. Had he been wrong about the master's intentions? Was this the moment when history would be made? His heart beat faster in his chest.

The man dismounted the donkey, taking in the scene, feeling the tension in the air. He spoke with dignity and authority.

149

"My friends," he called out, "this is a day of celebration. What we have all witnessed here has moved me greatly. God, our Father, has seen that the love of his people is strong. All the Angels have joined you in praise. He does not want blood to be spilled in my name. Nor does he want a hair of any child's head to be harmed. The happiness you have felt today you should carry in your hearts always. So, my friends, return to your homes and spread the news. God's Kingdom is coming but only He knows when. It will be at a time of His choosing, not mine. Return to your loved ones and celebrate the saving of the Children of Israel in Egypt this Passover. Go in peace and may God be with you always. So be it."

Turning to the soldier, he smiled. "Do you have your answer?" The crowd began to melt away and the troops dispersed. Many people were convinced they had seen the face of the Messiah on this day to remember. It was a story to tell their children and grandchildren. Others were unsure about the man being a king but had enjoyed the spectacle anyway. Everyone was happy that the event had ended peacefully, without any trouble to mar the holiday.

The disciples looked relieved. Fighting had never been part of their plan, although each had said he would be willing to lay down his life for the master. They too would leave and stay overnight with friends or family, promising to meet up the next day at the Temple steps. Only Judas felt disappointed and cheated. Once again he had been let down by this man, whom he had called 'Master' and 'Lord', who had come so close to being proclaimed King of the Jews and reuniting Israel. He was bitter and silently vowed to go ahead with his plans for handing the Master over to the priests.

"Let them sort it out," he said to himself.

Caiaphas breathed a sigh of relief when he heard the outcome. A riot had been averted and he could proceed with his own plans for this man's fate. His only hope was that it could be arranged to have the threat to his livelihood removed before Passover Day, after which time the crowds would leave Jerusalem and life would return to normal.

Maryam bade farewell to them all and went to visit her friend, Joanna, in her quarters at the palace of Herod Antipas. She promised to meet with him again at Martha's house in Bethany. Mary and all her family were staying with Joseph of Arimathaea, who lived in a large house with a courtyard near to the palace of the old, long since dead, King Herod, so called 'The Great'. Now the palace was the official residence of the Governor of Israel, Pontius Pilate. Joseph was a shrewd and successful businessman, owner of a small fleet of trading ships and a devout Jew. Most of the people he dealt with, both inside and outside Israel, were not of his religion. This made observing the multiple laws of the Sabbath difficult, especially when he was at sea. He was a kind and generous man. No one was ever turned away from his door hungry or empty handed. He traded mainly with the Romans, bringing in their supplies. He was always honest and fair, so they respected and trusted him.

He had kept in touch with Mary since her husband died and cared deeply for her son, as if he was his own, teaching him many things when they travelled together. He was not surprised that the teenaged boy turned out to be such a charismatic leader, loved by all who followed him.

After a simple, but delicious meal of goat's cheese, bread and fresh fruit, washed down with the juice of crushed pomegranate jewels, the family retired for the night, exhausted by the events of the day. Joseph took the man to his room, which doubled as his office when he was not at sea. It was decorated with mosaics of ships and seascapes. His table was covered with charts and lists of goods to be transported. He gave his nephew a goblet of wine and began to reminisce. They filled in the gaps of the time they had been apart.

The man brought up the subject of the place near Ephesus and Joseph promised to see John and Mary to safety. He also vowed to take Maryam away, probably to Gaul or Britannia, when he was told of her 'secret'.

"Are you sure you want to go through with all this?" he asked. "Aren't you afraid of death and the way you say it must happen?"

"People keep asking me if I am sure," he sighed, "and the answer is always the same. It is the will of God that I should suffer and die taking the sins of the world with me and that I should do it willingly. I thought earlier today that this might be the time but not with the possibility of all those people being massacred. If I thought there was another way I would take it but this is my destiny. It will be soon, though, tomorrow, or maybe the next day. My enemies are close." He paused and took a sip of wine, then continued, "In answer to your second question, no, I am not afraid of death. It is not a door closing but a door opening."

They discussed what might happen afterwards. "My followers will be hunted, so they will be afraid and run away. I have told everyone that the Temple will be destroyed and built again in three days," he said. "They hear my words but have not yet grasped the meaning. I will die, yes, but in three days I will rise again. This has been promised by God.

"There is one thing you can do for me Jofa. I have said that I do not fear death, although I am not looking forward to the agony of crucifixion. What I do not want, however, is to be left hanging on the cross until my eyes have been picked out by carrion crows and my feet torn to pieces by wild dogs. Promise me Jofa, you will somehow get me down and bury me before that happens. I don't want to become just another set of bones littering Golgotha. It is too far to bury my body in Nazareth and I do not want that anyway."

Joseph was close to tears, he was full of sadness and love for the man before him. "I'm not sure how," he gulped, "but I promise, on my life I will find a way. The actual burial place is no problem. I have one already, set up in a cave. It is prepared for my family when the time comes. I would rather be buried at sea, myself, but just in case... It is ready. Getting you there could be tricky but have no fear, I promise you, in God's name, it will be done."

They finished their wine in silence, each one was thinking of the days ahead. They spoke a little more, then embraced each other possibly for the last time and retired for what was left of the night.

The man and Mara shared their thoughts for a few moments, professing their love for one another and looking forward to seeing each other soon. Then they both slept, feeling the warmth of each other's arms around them.

The next morning the city was calm, everything was back to normal. After eating, Mary went round the market looking at all the cloths, especially the fine silks from beyond Arabia, then went visiting friends she had not seen for a year or more. Joseph spent some time working at home then went to see a business acquaintance to take his order for his next voyage.

As promised, the man went to the Temple to meet with his friends. His brothers James and Jude went with him, "To keep you out of trouble!" they joked, but they too were followers and were saddened when they learned of his fate.

Some of his disciples were already waiting for him and he joined them on the steps, remembering the first time he had come here as a boy. How things had changed. The number of traders and street sellers had more than doubled and the shouting of their wares was almost unbearable. Instead of lawyers and scholars sitting on the main steps, enjoying the sunshine and their philosophical discussions, there were beggars and cripples in their droves, forbidden to enter the

Temple as they were considered contaminated and unclean. Groups of vendors with sacrificial pigeons or lambs were doing a great trade and the shekels were piling up. Money changers were legion. Jews from foreign lands were changing their local currency into shekels then once more into Temple coins. These were silver coins, specially minted in the city of Tyre, bearing the image of the Emperor Tiberius, which were by law the currency used to purchase sacrifices. Each transaction cost the seller commission thus reducing the value of his money. The money men took their commission. The priests took their cut and the Romans took their taxes. Bribery and corruption was rife.

One poor wretch, a widow, pulled the last gold coin from her bracelet, no doubt the last of her dowry, in order to change it for enough to buy a small pigeon. The fat usurer first bit into the coin with his blackened teeth then put it on the scales to find its value. He flung the coin back at her feet, laughing disdainfully. "It isn't worth a pim!" he mocked. "Not even half a shekel. You had better go to work to earn enough for a pigeon, though who would want to buy your body I can't imagine!" Those around him laughed raucously as the poor woman scrabbled in the dirt to find her coin.

It was the last straw for the man seated on the steps. The sadness he had felt turned to frustration, and then the rage built up in him until he could stand it no longer. Jumping to his feet he seized a lash from the belt of one of the traders, who no doubt used it on his animals and began to yell.

He ran up the steps to the Royal Portico entrance roaring "NO, no, no. This is no longer a place of righteousness! This is no place to worship God! Get out, Go. Leave this place. Enough! You're all scum, vermin, thieves, liars, cheats," he screamed at the top of his voice, overturning tables as he ran, scattering piles of coins and scales.

Flailing his whip he scattered the pigeons into the air, squawking and losing feathers in their terror and adding to the chaos. The objects of his wrath cowered or fled the screaming madman, attempting to grab as much of their gold as they could, whilst escaping the stinging tail of the lash as it sniped and flailed above and below, snaking round table legs, overturning them, which scattered even more of the offensive coins around. Cups of wine and water shattered and spilled. The traders stumbled, ran, slithered and crawled in their attempts to escape down the steps.

Inside the Temple the sweet, cloying smell of smouldering resinous frankincense did little to hide the hideous stench of burning flesh. The piteous bleats of the lambs were silenced as the sacrificial knife sliced through their throats and their blood spurted into large, bronze bowls, before being slopped into gutters carrying it away to the open sewers where dogs lapped wolfishly. He grabbed a bowl and flung it into the air, drenching and spattering all those within its reach.

"May this blood be on you and your children's children," he screamed, rushing round, still lashing out with the whip. The priests and Pharisees around could only gape, open mouthed at the carnage surrounding them.

Outside, onlookers including the disciples and his brothers, were rooted to the spot in shock and horror. They could not believe what they were seeing and hearing. Some passers-by, delighted at the scene taking place in front of them shouted out their encouragement. This was even better than the excitement of the day before! They laughed and cheered, waved their arms, shouted and jeered at the retreating rabble of traders and usurers. Others looked on in dismay and anger at the thought of the Temple being defiled. Had God finally deserted them?

The wild man, spattered with blood, hair awry, finally halted. His anger sated, he seemed to be in a trance-like state.

He walked down the Temple steps, now deserted, with leaden steps as though his legs could hardly bear his weight any more. The crowd, now silent as they fixed him with their gaze, parted like the Red Sea as he walked through them and disappeared into the maze of cobbled streets surrounding the Temple.

Once again the disciples scattered into the crowd, fearing for their safety.

Maryam was distraught. She felt his anger and his pain. She sent calming thoughts to him. "Come to me Yeshi," she entreated. "I will ease your pain. Come, my love, rest in my arms and I will heal you,"

"No better place on earth," he responded.

CHAPTER THIRTEEN

The Last Supper

Martha studied the kitchen, mentally preparing the evening meal like a general preparing to go into battle. This was the Passover week of family holidays and celebrations. Thousands had already come to Jerusalem and the surrounding villages with more still to arrive. Nobody knew how many friends, neighbours or business acquaintances would stop by to say 'Hello' and stay for something to drink or eat and maybe for the dancing in the evening. It surely was one big organisational headache, one that she could not (would not) entrust to anyone else. Her sister, Mary, was useless in the kitchen and her brother Lazarus, perhaps wisely, was nowhere to be found. He was, no doubt, with his all his friends, praying, preaching or 'Hosannahring' somewhere between here and Jerusalem.

With all her familiar things around her, pots, pans, platters, clay oven, jars of wine from their own vineyard, sharp knives, cloths et cetera, Martha was content. Nothing could go wrong. Her routines were well practised and would be perfect. Her servants knew her requirements even to getting out of the way if, heaven forbid, something did go wrong. It hardly ever did but she had a harsh tongue and waspish ways if she was not altogether together satisfied, or was tired.

"Martha could out-breathe a dragon when she really gets going," they declared – behind her back of course!

A kid had been butchered, lamb was kept for the Passover meal itself. Bread was baking in the clay oven and delicate sweet pastries were soaking in honey, piled high on huge trays. Fruit, sprinkled with water to keep cool and fresh, was spread on woven baskets placed on high shelves to keep away from the sun. Similarly candied fruits, preserved in honey were arranged on platters to be eagerly pounced on.

The fire-pit in the yard was ready for lighting, waiting to cook the kid to perfection. Martha could almost smell the sweet aroma of roasting flesh and her mouth watered in anticipation. This was her day, nothing and nobody could spoil it. As she went through her lists in her mind, a shadow filled the doorway. Martha scowled and called out,

"Who is it blocking the light? Either come right in or go away. I'm busy."

The visitor chuckled, strode across the straw covered floor grabbed her by the waist and lifted her off her feet.

"Martha, you're beautiful when you're angry," laughed the master. "I've just come to say that supper tonight will be in Jerusalem, not here in this house but I still want you to do the preparations and to be in charge."

"No!" she retorted crossly, pushing him away "Impossible. Jerusalem is packed to overflowing at this time of the year. There isn't a place big enough for everyone that has not already been taken. It can't be done, sorry."

The man perched himself on the edge of the sturdy wooden table, shooing away a chicken which had wandered inside looking for some delicacy no doubt hidden in the straw. He turned his head slightly to one side with eyebrows raised, gave her an almost boyish, wheedling smile and fixed his twinkling eyes on her face.

"Oh most wondrous of housewives, it is already organised," he purred. "The Thunderers were sent out this morning with instructions to go to the market place and follow a man carrying a water jar on his shoulder to the house where they are, even as we speak, preparing the upper room for tonight's meal."

"Well!" snorted Martha, "it shouldn't be too difficult to find him. No man that I know of carries water pots. They usually leave that to their womenfolk. He will stick out like a fox in a hen house. But seriously my friend, is it safe for you to go back to Jerusalem? From what I heard, you nearly caused a riot in the Temple the other day. I wish I had seen it, though, all that money rolling round, birds squawking scattering their feathers, priests trying to catch them, people running every which way trying to escape. And you with that lash, ranting and raving, chasing the money changers down the steps. What were you thinking? No, you should not go back so soon. The priests will be angry and looking for a way to do you harm and Lazarus as well. They don't like the idea of anyone being raised from the dead. That's a step too far. It's just too dangerous. Besides it is all organised here." She waved her arms to show just how far her preparations had gone.

His eyes still on her, the master pushed himself off the table and moved towards her.

"I know it is dangerous, Martha," he agreed, nodding his head slowly and holding out his hands. "But it is very important that I am there tonight. In fact it is vital. These next few days will be very tense and fraught with danger. I cannot change what must be. You can do it, Martha. You are the strong one with enough love in your heart to put up with all of us for so long. You are the responsible, capable one. You are so organised you can do anything you choose. Besides, I can't see anyone daring to come for me when they spot you with that ladle in your hand!"

Already Martha's mind was marshalling her troops to transfer the foodstuff all the way to the city. "I hope this new place has a fire pit or it's bread and water for everyone," she yielded. "You are such a flatterer. Now get along with you – Cheeky!" She flicked her ladle at him and fine flour dust showered the air between them. Her hand flew to her mouth and her eyes widened as the powder settled on him. They were both stunned for a moment, then they both burst into laughter. She wiped tears from her eyes and held her sides.

"You have done so much for us, we can never repay you. You are someone very special, not just to us but to everyone. People say you are the Messiah, But I never imagined I would see the Son of God with flour in his eyebrows and beard!" she snorted again and tried to dab his face. He caught her wrist and gave her hand a big smacking kiss.

"You know, Martha," he beamed widely, "God is not always serious. He sees goodness and purity in happiness, laughter and even silliness. So, be happy, enjoy the good things in life. I certainly do, so be like me, believe in me and God's grace will be upon you."

"I do believe in you, especially after what you did for Lazarus." She waved the ladle in mock menace at him. "But, unless you can magic this meal to perfection, I've got things to do. So get along with you. Out of my kitchen."

He waved as he left to join Maryam in the garden.

"And another thing," she called to his retreating figure, "Where's my donkey!"

He found Maryam in the garden and they talked about all that had happened and what was to come. He had arrived back from Jerusalem exhausted, haggard, drained and sorely troubled by what had taken place at the Temple. He was shocked at his own violence. His actions were against all his

160

principles of turning the other cheek and loving his enemies. He had found Mara – at Martha's direction – in a shepherd's hut, a primitive shack made from branches covered with dried mud with woven reed matting on the earthen floor.

She had held out her arms and without saying a word he fell on her with need and desperation. Mara laid awake most of the night, whilst he slept fitfully, soothing, caressing and kissing away his troubled dreams. The next morning they made love with tenderness and passion and later still, with joy and happiness, until she felt that he was restored to his former, determined, self, strong as ever and more than willing to go forward to his destiny.

Now, he thanked her profusely, not knowing what he would have done had she not been there for him. They prayed together one last time, embraced sorrowfully and went their separate ways to prepare for the evening meal which they knew would be their last supper.

Later in the day the party of friends and disciples left Bethany, which for the master would be for the last time, to enter Jerusalem for their evening meal. They crossed the garden of Gethsemane along the Kidron valley to the southern gate of the city. In this way they were able to avoid the area round the Temple where they might be recognised.

Inside the gate was the pool of Siloam, filled with crystal clear waters from the Gihon spring. It was here that many blind, lame or paralysed, the so-called unclean sinners came to be healed. It was believed that when an angel passed by the waters would be disturbed and whoever stepped into the pool first would be cured. The master remembered the paralysed man who had been brought to the pool every day for over thirty years but had no one to put him into the water. Someone always got there before him but he had not given up hope. Taking pity on him, the master told him simply to stand up, pick up the mat he had lain on and walk away, cured and his 'sins' forgiven. Once again it had been the Sabbath on which day it was forbidden to carry a mat. The master smiled remembering the priest had been more concerned about the man carrying his bedding than the miracle of being cured.

Before even entering the upper room, where the meal was to be eaten, they could smell the roasted meat and chickens and hear the joyous sounds of music, chatter and laughter. The room was filled with friends, family and neighbours, all of whom had brought something to supplement the feast provided by Martha. The long, low tables were laden with jugs, platters, trays, copper dishes and clay bowls, each filled with delicious food. There were stuffed vine leaves, chicken, roast kid, fruit sweet pastries, bread and wine.

Everyone was in high spirits, meeting and greeting each other, catching up on the gossip and family news. They were happy at their reunion after long, tiring journeys now rested and relaxed they could tell stories of healings and miracles but no one mentioned the incident at the Temple. The menfolk sat on benches with cushions, whilst the womenfolk served, cleared the tables, played with the children, danced, sang, gossiped or just enjoyed being there. People came and went until the meal was finished when the women took their children home or cleared the debris from the tables and took their leave.

As Maryam left the room she caught his eye. "I don't want to leave you, my love. Not now, not ever," she signalled. "But I love you enough to let you go and do what must be done. Goodbye my love, my lord, until we meet again, in this world or the next."

"Mara," he messaged back to her, "we are never apart. We are as one. Do not grieve for me, there is no need. You are the last and the first. Take care, my love, of yourself and of Sophia. I will watch over you both. Go in peace." A tear trickled down her cheek as she turned to join the women.

Left alone, the disciples talked quietly amongst themselves. They knew the time had almost come for the master to leave them. He had told them of his death, why it was necessary and that it would be soon, although they did not quite seem to comprehend the enormity of it all. His mission was almost at an end, he had accomplished all he had set out to do apart from the one last phase. The Kingdom of God was almost here and nothing could stop him now.

He took a bowl of water and a cloth, proceeding to wash the dirt from the feet of the disciples. "What are you doing?" demanded Peter. "You are the Son of God. It is not fitting that you do such a menial task," to which the master replied,

"The Son of Man came, not to be served, but to serve others and to give his life for the sins of the people, all the people on this earth."

Later he took a round of unleavened bread and blessed it, as usual. Then he broke it into pieces. "Moses," he mused sombrely, "gave bread to the people coming out of Egypt and it saved their bodies. This bread will save the soul." He gave each of them a small piece. "This symbolises my body. Think of me whenever you eat it." There was a stunned silence and all eyes turned to him but he had not yet finished.

He took a cup of wine and once again blessed it. "This wine is my blood of the new covenant. Whoever drinks it in my name, will never thirst again." Passing the cup to each of them to take a sip, they said, "So be it." As he came to Judas, he withdrew the cup and narrowed his eyes. "Not you, Judas, you have work to do. Go. Do it quickly." Judas hesitated then nodded his head, understanding.

Judas of Karioth left the upper room going straight to the nearby house of Caiaphas. The guards tried to stop him but he brushed them aside and burst into Caiaphas' private rooms calling out,

"It is time. It must be this night!" He told the High Priest the route the Master would take, after the supper was finished. He then withdrew the purse Caiaphas had given him. "I don't want these pieces of silver. They are tainted Temple coins to be used to buy sacrifice. God doesn't want that and neither do I. Take them back!"

Caiaphas' eyes darkened and glinted with malice. "I cannot take them back," he shrugged. "They are payment for your services. Do with them what you will. Now, wait until I summon the captain of the guard. He and his men will accompany you to identify the man. After that, your part is finished and you are free to do whatever you think is right." Caiaphas left Judas for a while pondering over whether he had done the right thing already.

The disciples dispersed after supper leaving Peter, Andrew, James and John to accompany the Master back to Bethany. They re-crossed the Kidron Valley and stopped in the garden of Gethsemane at the foot of the Mount of Olives to rest and pray. The man took himself a little way apart from the others. He told them to keep watch for him but with full stomachs and having drunk copious wine their eyes were heavy and soon they slept.

The finality of what was to come, hit the man hard and filled him, once again, with self-doubt and dread.

"What if it all goes wrong? Does it have to be this way? Is this what God really wants? What about me and what I want?" Blood surged through his body, his pulse quickened as his heart beat faster, until he felt his head would burst. A cold sweat broke out on his skin and he shivered in fear. "Am I really the son of the Almighty, or has my whole life been a lie? What would my life be like if I ran away right now? Everything I've worked for would be lost. Those who followed and believed in me will call me traitor, fraud, the devil himself. There would be no resurrection or afterlife for me in heaven.

The priests would have won and God's people will be lost forever. May be the Kingdom of God depends on my death – so be it Father – my beloved abba. Not my will be done but yours. I will not doubt or let You down again'.

He was alerted by the light of flickering torches wending their way through the olive grove towards him in the gathering dusk. Quickly he went back to the others only to find them sleeping and angrily shook them awake. "Couldn't you stay awake for me for one hour?" he cried. "This is it! It is time. They have come for me!"

Stumbling to their feet, still groggy from sleep and wine, the four disciples were vaguely aware of Judas embracing their master, then being surrounded by armed guards. Finally stung to action, Peter drew his large fish gutting knife and sprang at the guard who had his hand on the master's shoulder. "No. Leave him alone!" he shouted and slashed at the captor, slicing off part of his ear. Blood spurted down the guard's neck.

The Master restrained Peter from doing further damage and so giving cause to be arrested himself. "Those who live by the sword, will die by the sword," he admonished his enraged disciple. Turning to the guard, he touched his ear and the blood flow ceased, the skin healed over as though nothing had happened. Only the bloodstains on his clothes served as a reminder of Peter's actions.

"I am the one you seek. I will go with you. Leave these others alone. They have done nothing wrong." The guards sheathed their swords and the disciples fled in terror. They feared that they would be hunted down as a follower in an attempt to eradicate the whole movement.

The guards tied the master's hands and marched him back to the house of the High Priest where Caiaphas was eagerly waiting.

CHAPTER FOURTEEN

The Trials

As High Priest in his first term of office, Caiaphas knew that it was imperative to maintain the semblance of peace, especially at this important time in the Jewish calendar. All Jewish people celebrated Passover in thanks for their time in Egypt, when the Angel of Death visited the land. They had been warned by Moses to kill a lamb and on the fourteenth day of the first month to daub its blood over the frames of the doors where they were eating. On that night the Lord sent a plague to punish the gods of Egypt by killing all the first born children and animals but passed over all the houses where the sign of the blood was painted. This special day had been commemorated for centuries. It was a joyous time when all families got together for a week long holiday. It also meant that thousands of people came to Jerusalem and the city was filled to overflowing.

Caiaphas, as had his father-in-law Annas before him, had been appointed by the Roman governor, Pontius Pilate. As well as presiding over the Temple proceedings, Caiaphas was responsible for the workings of the Sanhedrin. This was a court of law, consisting of priests, lawyers, judges and scribes, with jurisdiction over major crimes against the Laws of Moses. It was the High Priest who had control of the city, overseen by the Roman Prefect. If he failed in his duties, he would be relieved of his office and join the rank and file of Temple priests, a situation that he could not countenance. He had power over life and death and could order death by stoning or burning of a convicted criminal. He was indeed a powerful man.

He hated this man from Galilee, this upstart who threatened his authority, his practices and his future. How dare he forgive sins? Only God could do that, Could it also be true that he had raised a man from the dead? Were all the stories of healings and miracles true? He had prevented one riot in the streets when the man had ridden triumphantly into the city on a donkey but could he be sure he could control the situation over the next few days? This man, so revered in Galilee, must be stopped, permanently.

Caiaphas had thought long and hard about how he would achieve his aim. A trial was necessary but what would the charge be? Who would bear witness against the prisoner – false or otherwise . Could it be done before Passover Day? Should he be the one to pronounce sentence? What would the consequences of his actions be? So many things could go wrong and as yet he had no answers. He was only certain that this problem must be solved if he was to retain office and his extravagant lifestyle.

The captain of the Temple guard tugged roughly at the rope tying the prisoner's hands and pulled him to the foot of the dais where Caiaphas sat on a throne-like chair in the room where he met with dignitaries, petitioners, and fellow priests. The High Priest eyed the prisoner disdainfully.

Well, he thought, this country bumpkin looks as though he is easily intimidated. The man stood quietly before him, he seemed unperturbed, almost resigned to his fate. It was only when he raised his head and looked straight into Caiaphas' eyes that the inquisitor felt a shiver of apprehension run through his body.

"Who are you?" he asked, hoping for an incriminating answer such as "I am the Son Of God" or "I am the Messiah, the Christ, King of the Jews" but his hopes were dashed at the reply.

"You know who I am or you would not have arrested me."

"I know you are a rabbi and have been preaching throughout the country. Tell me, what is it exactly that you preach?" Again Caiaphas tried to get the man to condemn himself out of his own mouth, so that he himself could be the witness to the crime of blasphemy.

"Ask those who have heard me. I have done nothing in secret," the prisoner replied, where upon the guard struck him forcefully. "Show some respect," he ordered. "Don't speak to the High Priest in this manner!" The man's eyes flared as he rounded on the guard.

"If I have spoken lies, bear witness to the wrong. If I have spoken the truth, why do you strike me?" The guard was about to strike him again for insolence but Caiaphas held up his hand.

"I know it is late, but call on as many members of the Sanhedrin as possible for an emergency meeting within the hour," he commanded. "Secure the prisoner until the trial begins." The guard retreated to the courtyard and handed the man over to a soldier for safe keeping then taking several men he hurried to call on the members of the Sanhedrin, as ordered.

Annas, Caiaphas' father-in-law, had been listening to the proceedings. He stepped out of the shadows of a column. "Careful," he warned, "this 'trial' as you call it, will not be legal. There will be no witnesses or scribes to validate it. Everything must be open and above board or it may spark the very riot you are trying to avoid. It would be better for us if the blame for the man's death could be laid at the door of the Romans, not ours."

Caiaphas thought about this for a few minutes then said, "Maybe you are right. Let us see what happens at the Sanhedrin, then, I will decide."

Together, the two men and their bodyguards made their way through the narrow streets lit by flaming torches to the courtroom as part of the Temple precincts. A number of the members of the court had assembled, grumbling about being called from their evening meal or their beds.

What could be so important that they were called upon at this time of night? they wondered. Quickly, Caiaphas told them of his fears, explained what it was he required of them and why. "We need a 'guilty' verdict by whatever means possible," he told them sombrely. "It is essential that his man is removed from the scene as quickly as possible, or there will be blood running in the streets and out positions will be undermined."

When the prisoner was brought before them they bombarded him with questions. They taunted and mocked him but he said nothing in reply. They became frustrated and angry at his reluctance to answer. Eventually, Caiaphas' patience ran out.

"Are you the Son of God, the Messiah? Tell us," he boomed. Everyone held their breath. The silence was palpable. The man raised his head, smiled and spoke for the first time.

"If I told you, you would not believe me. I will tell you that the Son of man will sit at the right hand of God Almighty."

"Then you ARE saying that you are the Son of God?" shouted the High Priest, his heart pounding. This is it, he thought, this is where he condemns himself.

"Your words not mine, but you are right," the prisoner stated firmly.

Caiaphas became apoplectic and screamed to the gathered throng, "We do not need other witnesses. We have all heard him speak blasphemy. This warrants the death penalty. What do you say? What is your verdict?"

The angry Pharisees as one yelled back, "Guilty! He deserves death." Some threw their hands in the air excitedly, others gathered round the convicted man shoving, jostling him, even punching him or spitting at him. "Come on then Son of Man, who just touched you? You who know everything, strike him down." They continued to torment him until Caiaphas, triumphant but eager to be finished for the night, still elated by his success, called the meeting to an end, asking them all to return early the next morning to finish their business.

"Take him away," he ordered. "Sentencing will take place tomorrow, as the law dictates."

As the prisoner was led away, Annas spoke urgently to his son-in-law. "Don't be too hasty," he warned. "You cannot have him stoned to death, as the so called 'trial' is not strictly legal. There were no scribes present to record the proceedings. All the Galileans will be up in arms at the underhand way you have gone about this. They will demonstrate against the Temple and there will be trouble. You must take your fears to the Governor. Tell him you find the man guilty of subversion and let him pronounce the death sentence. The charge should be political not religious or else he will throw it back at you. His death should be soon. To keep him over Passover, which is in three days' time, is not acceptable and does not suit our purpose. Let the Romans take the blame and the consequences."

Caiaphas, still simmering with excitement, saw the sense of Annas' argument and agreed to go to the governor early the next morning.

Peter had followed his master, at a safe distance, from Gethsemane where he had been arrested, to the house of the

High Priest. Later, at a discrete distance he followed the guards as far as the Temple precincts to find out the outcome of his arrest. As he waited, warming his hands by the fire in the courtyard, a servant girl saw his face in the glow of the flames.

"Weren't you with that prisoner they brought in earlier?" she asked.

"No, not me," he replied shaking his head.

Another man sitting by the fire remarked, "Well you sound like him. Same accent and you're from Galilee so you must know him or have heard him preach."

"I tell you," Peter retorted, "I have never met him." A little later one of the guards walked by. He looked at Peter with a puzzled frown, then with recognition.

"You were in the garden of Gethsemane with him when he was arrested. Didn't you attack one of the soldiers? You are one of his followers."

Rising quickly, as the guard advance towards him, Peter backed away and shouted angrily, "You don't know what you are talking about. I do not know him!" At that moment the guards were called to accompany Caiaphas back to his home and others to take the man to his prison cell for the night, so Peter was left alone. Just as the man passed by, the cock crowed, he caught Peter's eye and raised an eyebrow, as though asking a question.

Peter, realising that he had done exactly as the Master had predicted, fled into the night, fearful of arrest and despairing of how, once again, he had failed his beloved Lord. "I don't deserve to live," he berated himself as he disappeared into the darkness.

The prisoner was lowered into a deep pit with a grill across the top for the rest of the night. He pulled his cloak tightly round himself and thought through the events of the day, from making love to his beloved Mara, his exchange with Martha, his last supper with his friends and families, the consecration of bread and wine, arrest, trial and finally his death sentence. The stone had been set to roll down the hill and nothing could stop its progress. His fate was sealed. He sent his thoughts to Mara, reassuring her that he was well, for now and in good spirits. He urged her to keep safe, trust in God and repeated his love for her. He spent a long time praying for strength and reassurance. Then he curled up as best he could at the bottom of the pit and slept intermittently.

The next morning, just after daybreak, a rope was lowered and he was hauled out of the pit, blinking in the bright sunshine. He was given a piece of unleavened bread to eat and a cup of water. He had his hands retied and was led away. He was taken, not back to the Sanhedrin as he had expected but to the courtyard of the Roman fortress where he was handed over to Roman soldiers for custody. It was here that he would stand before the Prefect of Judea, one known as Pontius Pilate.

Appointed by the Emperor Tiberius himself, Pilate was to govern this part of the Roman Empire. On arrival, he had angered the Jewish population by marching his soldiers through the Temple itself carrying standards bearing the image of Caesar Tiberius. He imposed heavy taxes in order to build roads, aqueducts and fill Tiberius' coffers. He also took bribes for favours to fund his own extravagant life-style. Anyone refusing to pay, or protesting was swiftly dealt with, trampled to death by horses, killed by the sword or lance or crucified on trees by the roadside as an example to others. Their crime, usually 'sedition' was written on a board above their heads.

It was Pilate's main task to keep the peace in this subjugated corner of the Empire, so any disturbance, riot or uprising, real or imaginary, was quickly quelled, often brutally.

He was surprised that a delegation from the Sanhedrin, led by Caiaphas, had requested an urgent meeting so early in the morning and only agreed to it because he was intrigued. Even earlier Caiaphas and Annas had met with the other court members and persuaded them that the decision they made last night was a hasty one and, it could be argued, not legal. Therefore, in order to achieve their aim, it was the Romans who must be seen to give the 'guilty' verdict. They had had to change the charge from blasphemy which was a religious matter, to a political charge of threatening the stability of the area, by an anarchist claiming to be the new King of the Jews. This was sufficient to warrant a hearing by Pilate who would be persuaded, or bribed, to issue the death sentence.

Until a couple of days ago, when a disturbance in the Temple was reported, Pilate had never heard of this person. In respect of the Jewish purity laws, he met with the priests outside his rooms at the fortress, in a small inner courtyard and listened to the charge. He was not a tall man, but with an ample girth draped in a white toga, leather boots up to his knees, short dark, well-trimmed hair and a gold badge of office round his neck. He ordered that the man be brought before him for interrogation. He studied the man claiming, potentially, to be the King of the Jews and was intrigued by him. He did not grovel, beg or weep as many who stood here before him had done. Nor did he rant and rave, citing the ills and crimes of the oppressors, vowing curses and terrible punishments upon them. The prisoner stood erect, calm and quiet, staring straight in front of him, no doubt resigned to his fate. He certainly did not look an 'evil doer' as the priest had said, nor did he look as though he was 'possessed by the devil' another accusation by them.

"What is your hurry?" he inquired of Caiaphas, who explained their fears of a riot over Passover if they ordered the accused man's death. "What is his crime?" was the next question.

"He does not pay his taxes and claims to be the King of the Jews, who will unite all the people of Palestine."

Pilate was not convinced that the Jewish leaders were concerned about one man not paying his taxes but claiming a kingdom was another matter entirely. He circled the prisoner saying ,"I understand you tell people not to pay taxes. Is this true?"

"I tell them to give Caesar that which belongs to him and to God everything else."

"I am also told that you claim to be the King of the Jews. What do you say to that?"

"It is true that I am of the line of King David. I am as you say but my Kingdom is not of this world. It is in the hearts and souls of the people."

"It seems to me that your own elders fear you more than I, so I will send you back to them."

The prisoner looked taken aback and startled. He started to speak but Pilate had already left to return to Caiaphas and his entourage. "I find no fault with this man on both the charges you have brought." He told them. "Deal with him yourselves. His 'crimes' as you call them are more spiritual than secular or political, so he is your responsibility."

Caiaphas seethed with fury but kept himself in check. "He has stirred up the people with his preaching and actions all the way from Galilee, through Judea and now into Jerus..."

"From Galilee you say?" Pilate interrupted. "Why didn't you tell me before? It should be Herod Antipas who tries him, not me. As Tetrarch of Galilee, he has the power to try and execute prisoners." With a sigh of relief, Pilate ordered that the accused be taken to the king's palace in the city, where Herod was staying for Passover.

The prisoner was worried. This was not what was planned. This was wrong and not how the prophesy was told. Herod did indeed have the power of execution, by the sword, as he had rid himself of John the Baptist, or by strangulation, carried out by one of his soldiers in the prison area.

I must be very careful, he thought. I must not give him the slightest reason to put me to the sword.

News of his coming quickly spread round the palace. People filled the courtyard and halls in order to catch a glimpse of the man they had heard so much about. When they saw him they were puzzled. How was it that this country bumpkin, dressed in torn, dirty clothing claim to be a king?

Herod Antipas sat on his throne, a goblet of wine in one hand and stroking his beard with the other. Decked in fine clothing and many jewels, with a circlet of gold on his head, he surveyed the wretched figure in front of him. Is it John the Baptist come back to haunt me? he wondered. Is he really greater than Moses, as some people say?

"Well, what have we here?" he said out loud. "I have heard that you perform miracles. Do one now so that we may all see and believe" The man stood still, eyes closed and his head bowed. "No answer? Well then, show us how you heal the sick!" still no response. "Come on, man. Do something. Say something. Don't just stand there."

The man remained silent and still. More questions came from Herod, his courtiers and priests but from the man there was nothing, no assent, denial, a nod or shake of the head. Eventually, Herod grew frustrated and bored. There was no entertainment value in the prisoner. He made one final attempt to get a response.

"So, you are the King of the Jews. You don't look like a king. How about a king's robe to wear? Would that suit you? Make you more talkative?" Amid much mocking laughter, the bedraggled prisoner was draped in a sumptuous, purple cloak embroidered with gold and jewels. Although the man seethed with inner anger, he maintained his silent stance. Herod could find nothing for which he could convict the accused man, so he could not sentence or execute the prisoner. Like Caiaphas, he did not want to be seen to be the one who would be blamed for the man's death unjustly. John the Baptist's death had caused a lot of ill feeling and unrest. A wrong step here and the consequences could be dire. In frustration, he ordered his men to take the prisoner back to Pontius Pilate.

From a doorway of an upper room, Maryam had watched the proceedings carried out below with dread in her heart. 'Be strong, Yeshi. God protect you my love'.

Pilate seethed with anger when the Jew was returned to his jurisdiction. He knew that he was being manipulated by the priests, who flatly refused to take responsibility for the death of the prisoner and yet, they were adamant that he must be executed. Antipas, that jumped up snivelling little coward, had also failed to find a reason for the death penalty.

He studied the man who once again stood before him, dressed in a ridiculous cloak. He was impressed by the man's calm unwavering attitude. Pilate looked him in the eyes and saw gentleness and compassion, almost as if the prisoner was sorry to be the cause of his dilemma. The Prefect knew that the priests' worries were more selfish than concerned about Roman reactions but he also knew he had to balance his responsibilities to Rome with the tension in the city. He spoke with the man further but could find no evidence that he had any intentions of starting a rebellion or of sedition. Pilate felt no personal threat and in his heart he knew the man to be innocent of any crime for which he could convict.

Outside, in the courtyard, Pilate informed the High Priest that he could still find no fault with the accused, therefore he would order a flogging by way of appeasement and subsequently set him free. Caiaphas was enraged, so much so that he did something he never would have envisaged. He challenged the Governor, the Prefect of all Judea, Pontius Pilate, ruler and peace keeper in Jerusalem.

"You must sentence him to death." He hissed. "What if there is a riot and word gets back to Rome that you could have prevented it? What if whispers get to Emperor Tiberius about the money lining your pockets instead of his coffers? What about the bribes you have taken and favours received? Your tenure here would be shortlived. On the other hand, if this prisoner dies, there will be no riot, no adverse reports and your lifestyle will be secure for a very long time. Besides, I cannot see your problem. You've had many others put to death without even seeing them, what's one more to you?"

Taken aback by this verbal onslaught, Pilate narrowed his eyes and said, "I will sleep on it, but there is a way we can both avoid the blame for his death and that is to let the people decide. If they love him as much as you say, they will opt to free him when I give them the choice between him and some other convicted criminal. Now go and do not say another word." With a wave of his hand, he dismissed Caiaphas and ordered the guard, Roman this time, to secure the prisoner.

The soldiers lowered the man into a deep hole in the ground which served as a cell for the night. As darkness fell, the Centurion from Capernaum came to bring him some food and drink. He also brought him his own cloak instead of Herod's ridiculous mantle, for which the gentle man thanked him.

"I'm sorry to see you here, my friend." The Centurion spoke softly. "It is not right. Let us hope that tomorrow you will be free to go and can put all this nonsense behind you. The Prefect does not relish being pressurised by the priests. He will find a way to set you free but he must be careful to preserve the peace at this busy time of the year."

The man smiled wanly. "It is my fate to suffer for my beliefs," He told the Centurion. "If things go badly for me tomorrow, then I would ask you to contact a man well known by the Prefect. His name is Joseph of Arimathaea, a merchant who frequently advises Pilate on matters of trade and mining.

He and I have spoken and he knows my wishes. He will contact Pilate tomorrow, so please try to speak with him."

The Centurion agreed to speak with Joseph, then he left the man to try to sleep. He told the guards to treat the man well and to keep careful watch so that no one should approach him. He did not trust the priests who wished the prisoner harm.

The next morning Pilate, having slept badly, again entreated the priests to allow him to set the man free with a flogging but Caiaphas was adamant that the man should die. Pilate eyed him with a stony glare.

"I warn you priest, do not push me too far. The people will decide who dies and who is set free. It will be this man, who in my eyes has done nothing wrong, or an already convicted thief, terrorist, Zealot and murderer named Barabbas. To me there is no doubt who they will choose and you must accept their choice without question. Do I make myself clear?" Caiaphas acquiesced reluctantly but his mind was already racing as to how he could take advantage of the situation.

Pilate strode to the public courtyard and stood on the steps to address the gathering. Two men also stood on the steps, to one side. The first stood quietly with his head bowed, seemingly deep in thought. The second man, short and stocky, stood, hands akimbo, looking arrogant and defiant. While he waited for the crowd to quieten, Pilate thought of something that the Emperor had once said.

"People love violence and spectacle. To prevent them from being violent themselves, let them vent their feelings on displays of violence to others. Give them bread and circuses that they may be sated." Pilate had heard of huge arenas being built, where men, slaves or convicts would be pitted against wild beasts or each other in a fight to the death, whilst the crowd watched, cheered, booed, stamped, whistled or screamed for more blood.

He raised his hand for quiet and the crowd hushed expectantly. Soldiers lined the walls, eyes everywhere, ready to pounce on any troublemaker or quell a disturbance. Pilate cleared his throat.

"People of Jerusalem," he called out. "It is almost Passover day and in honour of this historic occasion I will exercise my right to free a prisoner to you. Here before you stand two men. The first is a Galilean, who, in my opinion, has done nothing wrong and has committed no crime in the eyes of the law. The second is a man already convicted and sentenced to crucifixion for insurrection, terrorism and murder named Barabbas. The choice is yours. What say you? The Galilean or Barabbas?"

Knowing what Pilate intended, Caiaphas had hastily arranged for several of his men to be scattered in the crowd that morning. There were a few people from Galilee who knew the preacher but many more who knew of the political zealot. At Caiaphas' signal one of his men shouted out,

"Give us Barabbas!" Other zealots, from Barabbas' own corps of men in the courtyard took up the cry. "We want Barabbas," they yelled. Soon more and more people joined in chanting. "Barabbas, Bara-bbas, Bar-ab-bas." Pilate was dismayed at their choice and made one more attempt to free the Nazarene.

"What of this man?" he almost pleaded. "He has done no wrong." The cry from the inflamed crowd was now for blood.

"Crucify him!" they bayed. "Crucify him." Pilate could see that nothing would change their minds. He saw the smug look of triumph on Caiaphas' face and turned away angrily. Taking water from a nearby bowl he washed his hands so that all might see him cleansing himself of any blame for the death of an innocent man.

The Centurion, his face darkened with disbelief, ordered the courtyard to be cleared by the soldiers.

Pilate turned to the man with regret. "I'm sorry," he said resignedly. "There is nothing more I can do. The sentence must be carried out immediately." To his surprise the man seemed to grow in stature and smiled at him, almost with satisfaction on his face.

"It is my destiny," was all he said as he was led away by the captain of the guard, the same one he had confronted on the Via Dolorosa several days ago.

"I knew you were trouble as soon as I set eyes on you," he grunted. "I just didn't think we would meet again so soon."

There followed a flogging, laying stripes across his back as he was tied to a post, watched disinterestedly by soldiers who had witnessed such scenes many times before. He flinched each time the lash caught his flesh, biting his bottom lip to prevent himself from screaming, trying to cut his mind free from the bodily agony. Some of the rank and file stopped cleaning their swords and breastplates to come close and mock him. Bowing down before him they cried in false tones.

"Hail, oh King," then spat upon him. "He hasn't got a crown," said another. "You can't be a king without a crown." Then he proceeded to pull twigs from a nearby thorn bush and twisted them into a circlet which he then pressed onto the prisoner's head. They did not care that Pilate has pronounced him innocent, only that this was a sport which filled an otherwise boring routine day. The sharp thorns pierced the skin on his forehead so that blood dribbled over his face, into his eyes and down his neck. As a final insult the soldier who had administered the flogging, threw a bucket of cold water over the poor wretch's back.

Following routine procedure, the execution squad released him from the whipping post and dragged him to where heavy wooden poles were stacked against a wall. Each one was a parabellum or cross post onto which the prisoner would be nailed. All of them had been used in the past, as had the nails which were expensive and in short supply. When everything was in place, it was now the fifth hour of the day, the post was laid across the man's shoulders and the macabre procession set out along the uphill climb to the place of execution, to Golgotha, the place of the skulls, littered with many bones of unclaimed victims of crucifixion.

Most of the spectators had gone by now, just a few remained, huddled together in one corner of the courtyard. His mother, favourite disciple and his beloved Mara had witnessed everything and now stood sobbing, ashen faced or just staring in stunned disbelief.

There was one other, hidden by a stone column – Judas of Karioth. The finality of what had just taken place filled his soul with self-loathing. It was never intended that his master should be put to death.

'What were his last words to me?' he thought. 'You will be remembered throughout history. It is all my fault. I have betrayed the Son of God. There is nowhere for me to hide, especially from myself. Christ I am sorry! God forgive me'. He hurriedly left the city and found a tree in a field where unclaimed bodies were interred. Taking off his own belt and letting his money bag spill on the ground, Judas, the freedom fighter, disciple of the Messiah, betrayer of his much loved friend and master, hanged himself by the neck until he was dead. Somewhere in the universe a shooting star crossed the heavens, momentarily sparkling, then disappeared forever.

CHAPTER FIFTEEN

Calvary

Crowds, once more, lined the streets of Jerusalem to catch a glimpse of the Nazarene, the so called holy man. Less than a week had gone by since there were adoring shouts of 'Hosanna', now there were only shouts of derision at this pathetic, broken man, bent under the weight of his burden. He was flanked by Roman soldiers who kept the crowds in check as they passed by. Some did not know who he was. To them he was a man convicted of a crime and sentenced to death, therefore he deserved to be jeered and spat upon. Many knew him but felt betrayed. He had promised so much and it had all come to naught. Others were silent, lowering their eyes and bowing their heads in shame and sorrow, praying silently and feeling the pain of the man as he struggled to keep his footing on the cobbles of the Via Dolorosa. His once beautiful cloak was now filthy and blood streaked. It trailed on the ground over the open sewers draining down the street.

His shoulders and arms jarred as the cross beam struck the walls of the narrow street. His back still stung from the strokes of the lash and his legs burned from his efforts. He felt his strength failing and stumbled. Without the use of his hands to steady him, he would have fallen had not a stranger in the crowd stepped forward to hold him. The stranger, Simon of Cyrene, had come to Jerusalem from far away Libya, bringing his young son for his first Passover. Simon took the weight of the cross on his own shoulders. The prisoner smiled his thanks with his eyes, his mouth too swollen and dry to speak. He silently thanked and blessed the stranger.

Later that day Simon told his family that the man seemed to radiate an almost tangible feeling of warmth, love and peace. It was hard to believe this man could have ever committed any sort of a crime, let alone one so evil it deserved the death penalty! He felt angry and frustrated when the yoke was wrested from his sturdy shoulders and placed once more on the frail prisoner. He felt like striking out at the soldier but was roughly shoved aside, back into the crowd and the procession passed him by.

A woman, he recognised as one whom he had healed months previously, stepped out of the crowd, tears in her eyes, and held a cup to his lips.

"Drink, Master," she whispered, "it will deaden the pain."

He gulped some of the liquid down, tasting wine mixed with the bitterness of myrrh. He nodded his thanks before she too was pulled away from him, spilling the rest of the wine.

Away from Pilate's fortress, the crowd thinned out. They were more subdued and felt sorrow for the man, he was after all one of their own countrymen condemned to death by the hated Romans and he looked so beaten. He did not beg for help or mercy as others had done before him and they admired him for that.

It was the middle of the day, the sixth hour when they finally reached the place of execution. The sun was at its zenith, blazing down from a cloudless blue sky. Spectators had gathered to watch the crucifixions. There were to be three of them on that occasion, two were pathetic, small time but persistent robbers and thieves and this man who claimed to be some sort of man of god and a King of the Jews, mad man more likely, they thought.

The uprights of the crosses were laid on the ground, each over a deep hole in which they would eventually stand once the victim was secured. Carrying out a crucifixion was a well-practiced routine for the soldiers of the execution squad. First, they lodged the cross beam into a slot at one end of the main post. Prisoners were then stripped of their clothing, which was tossed aside until they had time to check for anything worthwhile. The arms were stretched out along the beam and secured by ropes before the nails went in. Nails were expensive and in short supply, so were repeatedly used. It had been known that victims had literally torn their hands free of the nails in an attempt to escape, so the ropes lashed round their arms doubly made sure they stayed put.

There was a short bar across the upright for the prisoner to place his feet as the post was lowered into the hole. Soldiers supported the weight of the cross whilst it was stabilised with rocks, sand and stones. Another long nail was then hammered through the feet into the wood beneath.

The soldiers were oblivious to the agonised screams of the victim. They were just doing their job, one which no one volunteered for. After the routine search of discarded clothing or belongings, they divided their spoils and left the crucified ones to their inevitable fate.

The process of death was long, slow and painful. With no food or drink, the body soon lost its strength. The weight of the body put tremendous pressure on the shoulders and chest so breathing became laboured and difficult. Many died from asphyxiation, others just lost the will to live. Those who were determined to hang on to life as long as possible were helped on their way by having their legs broken or a sword thrust into their side. Even the strongest could not cheat the inevitable, but sometimes took up to three days before being officially declared dead.

On this occasion, the master lay on the beam on the ground, mentally preparing himself for what was to come. He took a long, last look at the beautiful sky above him then closed his eyes and mind to shut out the world.

"Soon it will be over, just a little longer to wait and I will be at peace with my Father in heaven," he consoled himself. He shut out the clamour of the crowd and the chatter of the soldiers as they went about their tasks. He felt the bite of the rope as it clamped his arms and was secured. He did not see the swing of the hammer as it drove the nails through the palms of his hands and the pain did not register for a few seconds. With a sharp intake of breath, he managed to stifle a scream, then realised that the nails had not crushed through any bones as they pierced his hands.

Another Prophesy fulfilled, he thought. Not a bone in his body will be broken. Everything is happening as foretold. Similarly, his feet were nailed to the post without touching a bone. He was aware of the screams of the victims on either side of him. They were cries of terror rather than pain.

As the soldiers hoisted the upright into the hole in the ground, he suddenly felt disoriented and had to fight to quell a feeling of nausea and tasted the bitterness of the wine and myrrh in his mouth. Strangely, he felt comfort from the ropes which pinioned his arms to the cross. Breathing became more difficult so he slowed his heart rate and waited for death.

The last task that the soldiers had to perform before raising the cross was to nail a sign above the victim's head, stating his crime. The words "'Robber' and 'Thief'" were written on the boards above the men on either side of the master but Pilate had personally ordered a special plaque with 'I.N.R.I' inscribed on it to be placed over this particular prisoner's head. The High Priest had immediately objected as it translated from the Latin 'Ieshua. Nazarene. Rex. Iudeorum into 'Jesus of Nazareth, King of the Jews'. Despite Caiaphas' protests Pilate was adamant.

"I have written what I have written. It stays."

Having completed their tasks, the soldiers turned once again to mock him.

"All hail, king of the Jews," then laughed as they sorted through the meagre belongings of the three men.

"Nothing much here," they complained. "Except for this cloak. It is dirty and torn but it is finely woven and good quality. It looks too good to be split up between us." They decided ownership of the cloak that Maryam had so lovingly fashioned, by throwing dice. The soldier with the highest number claimed it to be his own. The man nailed to the cross, raised his head and spoke.

"Father, forgive them, for they know not what they are doing."

The crowd on the hillside at Calvary still jeered at him. "If you are the Son of God, come down from the cross. Save yourself."

"Heal your own wounds!"

"Show us a miracle!"

Even one of the two men hanging on his cross, groaning in pain, said, "If you who they say you are, can't you get us all down?"

The other retorted quickly, "Shut up, you miserable worm. Have you no fear of God? We are getting what we deserve. We've been warned enough times. But him, he has done nothing wrong." Then addressing the master directly, he said quietly, "Sir, I do not expect you to forgive my sins, there have been too many. All that I ask of you is that you remember me when you enter your heavenly Kingdom."

The master smiled weakly and replied. "I tell you truly, tonight you will be in Paradise."

The soldiers settled down on the grassy bank to wait for other guards to relieve them of duty. Many of the crowd started to drift away, disappointed that there was no more spectacle or excitement, since the man had not responded to their taunts. They returned to their homes to prepare for the Passover Sabbath the next day and to relate to their friends and family what they had witnessed.

Although there were several hours before the end of the day, the sky began to darken with thick clouds gradually blotting out the light of the sun, until it was as black as night. A wind got up and howled across the hillside, lightning crackled and thunder rumbled. People gathered their clothes around them against the wind and became afraid.

"This weather is not natural," they said. "It is a sign from God. Something is very wrong here."

It was even more frightening that at that moment the Master called out in a loud voice,

"My God, My God. Why have you forsaken me?"

The onlookers waited expectantly. Maybe God would come from the skies, or Moses, or Elijah, Abraham himself possibly. Perhaps the man would be lifted from the cross and rise into heaven in a blaze of glory. Maybe they would all be struck down. What an extraordinary day this had been! After a while when nothing happened, they shrugged their shoulders and continued their way home, still battling against the wind.

The Centurion, who had been the overseer of the proceedings, took a long stick with a sponge tied to one end. He poured a liquid from a pouch at his waist onto the sponge. Lifting it to the man's lips he called softly,

"Drink this. It is vinegar to make you more thirsty, so your end will come quickly."

The master licked his parched lips with his swollen tongue and swallowed the sour liquid, again detecting myrrh and something he could not quite place, not that it mattered anyway. He felt light-headed and his arms and shoulders tingled as his blood drained and settled in his lower body. He was so tired. With enormous effort he opened his eyes and raised his head one last time. Vaguely he could just make out the figures of his mother, John his disciple and Mara standing a little way off. Rain was falling now. He could just make out their bedraggled shapes and felt so sad that he had caused them such pain. After what seemed to him an age he gathered his remaining strength, took in a deep breath and murmured,

"It Is Finished."

He lowered his head to his chest. The crown of thorns tumbled to the ground. His shoulders shuddered one last time and his body sagged. He had been on the cross only three hours.

Great flashes of lightning streaked repeatedly across the sky, silhouetting the line of crosses with their pathetic, sagging bodies. Almost immediately, great claps of thunder drowned every other sound with a deafening roar. The very earth shook and rocks dislodged, rolling down the hillside. Any remaining bystanders fled in terror.

The soldiers hastened to finish their tasks by taking clubs and breaking the legs of the two robbers to ensure their swift death. The centurion prevented them from doing the same to the third man.

"There is no need," he declared. "I have checked his body with my sword and no blood flowed. He is dead." Then, to himself he said, "You were truly the Son of God. Forgive me my friend." There was no response. The Centurion hurried back to report to Pilate, as ordered, the outcome of the day's events.

Maryam had waited, watched and listened throughout the day with Yeshi's mother and his young disciple John. They had been in Pilate's courtyard at the fortress, fully expecting him to be freed, since neither Caiaphas nor Herod Antipas was willing to sentence him and had returned him to the Prefect. He had stated that he found no fault with the man and no case to answer. She wanted to be there for him then take him home and care for him in Migdahl. She was filled with horror and loathing as the assembled crowd of her own countrymen had screamed for his death. She suddenly remembered the vision she had seen when she was in the wilderness with him. The sea of faces praising and adoring him one minute then those same faces changed to vile, evil tormentors condemning him and baying for blood. He had known even then that this would happen. She was utterly helpless and bereft as she watched him tied to a whipping post and flogged, mocked and spat on. The three of them tried to get close as he was led away but were forced back by the soldiers.

They stood at the foot of the mound, called Golgotha, where the cross was erected. Mary was weeping and was being comforted by John, who had taken on the role of protector. Maryam stood stony faced, as he was nailed to the cross, stripped of his clothing and still with that ridiculous crown of thorns on his head. There was nothing she could do.

The midday sun had beaten down on his body, still striped and bruised from the cutting blows of the lash. He had a thin slick of sweat on his skin but his lips were dry and cracked. His lank hair hung over his face. The thorns had pierced his skin so the drops of blood had mixed with sweat and trickled down his face. The blood had dried now so the lines looked like crusted red maggots eating away at him. Those deep, brown, hypnotic eyes were closed now and forever. Never more would they crinkle with laughter, flash with passion or blaze with fury. Had she caught his look just before he gave up his spirit? She had tried to send her thoughts to him in one last message but there was no response.

The mouth that she had kissed so often was now hanging loose in a silent scream that only she could hear. It was tearing her apart! Those strong arms, now useless, sore and chafed from the ropes used to hold her, sometimes tightly, sometimes gently and those poor hands were torn and bloody from the ugly nails. What pain he must have felt. Every blow to them felt like a hammer hitting her own heart. He was not breathing any more.

He looks so broken, she thought. Maybe it is all finished like he just said. Has his soul joined with his spirit and risen to be with the Father? Why did it have to be like this?

Maryam wished she could cut him down right now, wash his tired feet, filthy from the trek from the fortress to this foul place. She wanted to breathe new life into him. She felt empty and heavy at the same time. Would she really see him again other than in her dreams? He had promised to be with her throughout all eternity. One hand rested on her heart, which she felt was broken, the other stroked her belly as if to protect the new life inside her.

Maryam had been aware of the darkening sky and the gathering storm but she had no thought of leaving him. Maybe it is just the darkness in my heart and mind, she thought. The people, who had come to watch the spectacle and jeer at him, were scurrying away now, ahead of the storm.

"I hope you all had a good time," she raged. "I hope you all enjoy your Passover with your loved ones. I hope you all rot in Hell!" She suddenly felt tired and drained. She had no energy to waste on anger.

"I should not curse them like that, should I?" she asked herself. "He said they should be forgiven because they did not know what they were doing. If he can forgive them then so can I. I'm such a bad person. It is all my fault. I could have tried harder to change his mind. We could have gone away together." She sighed, knowing that nothing she, or anyone else, could have said would alter his destiny.

Thinking about the others, she was resentful that all of them, except for John, had deserted him, not that there was anything they could have done but be there for him.

We are such a rag-tag group of misfits, she mused. We only bonded together in our love for him and what we thought was the right way of spreading his message of peace, love and understanding. Where did it all go wrong? Was it too much too soon, or too little too late? It does not matter now. They've all scattered like sheep, just as he said they would. There is nothing that they could have done except be there for him. Peter let him down, once more. I knew that he would. He was so jealous of me. I felt afraid of him when he drew his fingers across his throat with hate in his eyes. Andrew was always a follower, never a leader. James always wanted to throw thunderbolts at people. I never saw it happen. John so gentle, but always wanted to stay close to Yeshi. Philip and Nathanial were the intellectuals, always wanting 'the truth' and knowledge. They hardly had any time for the illiterate ones. As for dear Matthew, old habits die hard and they never really trusted him. I wonder where Simon went to? He was such a loner, always sneaking off to see his old friends. I wonder if he was pleased when his friend Barabbas was set free? Where did Judas go? Now, there is a man I never want to see ever again! I do not think I could ever forgive the son of a dog for betraying you Yeshi, even though you said it was his destiny.

Maryam broke from her reverie, realising that she was soaked to the skin. Mary and John were saying that they were about to return to the city. She promised to join them in a little while to help prepare the Passover meal. She did not think she would ever celebrate this event again. Left alone, she continued to stare at the lifeless body of her lover.

"I should go, like everyone else," she told him. "There is nothing for me here now." The rain was washing the blood from his body and the dirt from his feet into a pool at the base of the cross. The other two men, their legs bent in strange angles where their bones had been broken, were no longer breathing.

"God rest your souls," she sighed.

Maryam kissed Yeshi's feet as a final gesture then turned to walk down the stony path, littered with bone fragments, now running like a small stream. The soldiers, onlookers and family had all gone. The hillside was deserted.

This is strange, she thought. He should not be left alone. Someone usually guards the bodies for a couple of days. Maybe the storm has scared them away, or maybe they are celebrating ownership of a new cloak.

Momentarily, she thought of the cloth that she had woven with such love and care, of his pleasure when she first gave it to him. Sometimes he wrapped it round her when it was cold and then laughed at her as she tripped because it was too long. She could not suppress a smile and turned to see her beloved one more time. The smile froze on her face and her body turned to stone.

Someone was approaching the cross.

CHAPTER SIXTEEN

The Burial

Maryam stood stock still. What was happening? Someone was coming. Three men emerged from the gloom. She forced her leaden feet to retreat into the shadow of a tree so she could observe what was going on. She recognised the plumed helmet of the Centurion who had been in charge of the execution squad earlier today. As he came closer she saw him draw his sword and she had to stifle a scream that rose in her throat. She wanted to shout out to him,

"Get away from him. Don't touch him. Haven't you done enough for one day? Do you want to kill him all over again?"

Still rooted to the spot, the movement of the other two men caught her eye. They were pulling a small hand-cart. Instantly she recognised them as Joseph of Arimathaea and Nicodemus, both of whom she had spoken to at their last supper together, barely two days before. She did not understand what was going on but could not intervene.

Placing the cart at the foot of the cross and steadied by Nicodemus, the Centurion climbed onto it and expertly cut the rope behind the cross bar so there was no damage to the wrists. Joseph cut the rope binding his feet and rubbed some tincture into the wound, smelling of oil and myrrh. He firmly grasped the head of the huge nail and gently teased it out, grimacing as he did so. He took the weight of the body in his arms. Tears were flowing down his face mixing with the raindrops. His mouth was set in a straight line of determination.

The Centurion repeated his operation on the other arm, extracting the nails as carefully as Joseph had done. Nicodemus kept looking round fearfully, urging them to hurry.

"What if the soldiers or the Temple guards come back?" he whispered nervously. "We will be done for"

The Centurion laughed. "No way," he answered. "Not in this weather. It is coming up to Passover Sabbath, remember. Everyone is in their homes. There will be no disturbances tonight. My men have been given the night off and your Jewish traditions forbid anyone, least of all the Temple guards walking this distance on the Sabbath. Don't worry, we will be quite safe."

"Just get on with it," urged Joseph impatiently.

They lowered the lifeless corpse onto the cart and the Centurion covered it with his own cloak.

"It grieves me to see him like this. After what he did for my servant, I owed him a debt of gratitude. He told me that I would know if ever I could help him. There are still things to do so let's finish this."

Between them they wheeled the cart, rumbling and creaking down the stony path towards the place where Joseph had hollowed out a cave to form his family crypt. Maryam followed at a safe distance, quietly and hidden by the darkness so not to be detected. The rain had stopped but the clouds still covered the sky. Eventually, after much pushing and pulling, puffing and panting, their backs aching from the unaccustomed exertion, they arrived at the burial site. A cave cut into the rock, the walls smoothed and covered in a wash made from crushed limestone.

Inside the tomb were several ledges, waiting for the ossuaries of Joseph and his family in years to come. On the cave floor laid a marble slab on which the body was placed. The Centurion remained outside, not wanting to defile the site with his non-Jewish presence, said quietly,

"I will take my leave of you now. There are duties I must perform at the fortress and at Pilate's palace. I do not want to be missed and have to account for my whereabouts. Do what you have to do and farewell." He bowed his head for a moment as if in silent prayer and then disappeared into the darkness.

Joseph and Nicodemus carried the body reverently in to the tomb and laid it on the stone slab. Joseph lit several torches and oil lamps, the smoke from which curled up to the roof of the cave leaving sooty stains on the rock surface above.

It was then that Nicodemus came into his own right. As a trader in expensive oils, perfumes and spices, he had sold many concoctions for cosmetic, healing or embalming purposes. Dealing with dead bodies was left to the women folk but he knew exactly what to do and went about his task quickly and efficiently. Several jars, bottles and packets were brought from the pouch which hung from his belt. As the seals were broken a sweet fragrance filled the whole cave. Swiftly and deftly he poured oil along the length of the body and massaged it into the skin of his rabbi and friend, covering all the sores and wounds. Next he mixed herbs and crushed aloes with the juice of roots and rubbed the paste into the skin as a preservative.

"We should have brought some camel dung so that if any does check, the place will smell of decaying flesh," he mentioned. Joseph rolled his eyes and shook his head. He then continued to wrap the body in a soft, white cloth as a burial shroud. He used a separate cloth to cover the head. Spices were layered into the cloths to preserve the skin. When they were finished, they looked round, did a little tidying up and were satisfied with their efforts.

"I wish it was anyone but him," he said softly. "One day, I will lie here in my sleep and will see him again."

"Come on," urged Nicodemus. "We can't risk being seen down here and besides, it is nearly the Sabbath and we must get home. The women will be wondering where we are. I don't think I can stand being questioned and nagged by my wife tonight. I just want to get home, eat, drink and, if possible, sleep. Our work here is finished. I only hope this is the end of it. I do not want to be arrested by the Romans."

They stood in silence for a moment then walked back up the few steps to the cave entrance. Joseph secured the tomb by removing the wedge holding the boulder in place. With a creak and a rumble the stone slid along the channel at its base and came to rest in a cloud of dust, sealing the opening from predatory animals. They trudged wearily down the path, pulling the cart behind them, retracing their steps back to Jerusalem and solemnly promising each other not to mention their involvement to any other living soul.

Maryam left her hiding place and pressed her body against the boulder.

"Sleep well, my love. I know you are at peace now and with your Father. I will come again soon." She kissed her fingertips and placed them on the stone. Carefully looking round, she noted the exact location of his resting place, the path, the rock and the stubby shrubs nearby. Then, she too retraced her steps to Jerusalem, still wondering at what she had seen. Puzzled at what it all meant, she was determined to seek out Joseph and find the truth.

THE END OF THE BEGINNING

CHAPTER SEVENTEEN

Passover

The streets of Jerusalem rang with music and laughter as people enjoyed the festival commemorating the miraculous escape from the Angel of Death, so many years ago in Egypt. Families, friends and strangers alike greeted each other and joined in the merry-making. The day was fine and clear with no sign of the clouds which had darkened the sky on the previous day.

Following tradition, many had expressed their thanks by visiting the Temple, paying for their sacrificial gifts and making donations to the coffers. There was no sign of the disturbance earlier in the week. It was business as usual and everyone was happy. The priests were overworked performing their ritual slaughter of lambs, kids, doves and pigeons. Copious blood flowed down the channels to the outside drains, smoke rose to the sky and the smell of roasting meat drifted right across the city.

Caiaphas was content. Everything was back to normal, just as he had planned. There were no riots as people were too busy holding family reunions. The danger had been averted and the threat removed. Money was rolling in, sufficient to pay the Temple taxes to Rome with enough left over to keep him more than comfortable. He had slept well and was looking forward to the rest of his tenure as High Priest.

Today he would enter the Holy of Holies to commune directly with God and lay his hands on the Ark of the Covenant containing the Laws of Moses, written in stone. He was dressed in his finest, ceremonial raiment. His golden, bejewelled badge of office hung round his neck and his golden mitre was in his hand. He looked round with great satisfaction as he presided over the rituals of the day. As the ceremony reached its climax, he slowly and solemnly wended his way up the thickly carpeted steps to the small, square room that only he was allowed to enter. With annoyance he noticed that the richly embroidered curtain covering the Holy place was torn.

Who could have done this? he wondered. Heads will roll.

Putting aside his annoyance, he took the gold key from his belt and with a flourish he inserted it in the lock. Murmuring incantations he turned the key slowly and opened the door. One step inside was enough. His eyes swept the room and saw only devastation. The walls were cracked from roof to floor, the altar had crumbled and the Ark of the Covenant lay miraculously unscathed, on the floor. Panic surged through Caiaphas. Had God done this? Had some madman broken in causing such disaster? He remembered the storm of the previous afternoon and the earth tremor, neither of which was natural.

This was God's punishment for what he had done. Caiaphas staggered backwards and fell, rolling down the steps to a crumpled heap on the ground. Priests hurriedly carried him to his private chambers and summoned a physician.

Elsewhere in the city, Pilate paced up and down. He was restless and agitated. An abundance of red wine had not helped him to sleep. Bacchus had repaid him with a vile headache and a nauseous stomach. His wife kept giving him accusing looks which translated as 'I told you so'. The sound of metal on metal as soldiers clashed their swords in practice, the rhythmic pounding of marching feet and the shouted orders of the drill master, compounded his misery.

"Why do I feel so guilty?" he asked himself. "None of this was my fault." He just hoped that the soldiers would keep order in the city. He had been revisited late last night by Caiaphas, who had entreated him to post guards at the tomb. He feared that the disciples would make an attempt to remove the body and thereby fulfil the Prophesy that he would rise again on the third day. Pilate had tried to dismiss the High Priest with an unsteady wave of his hand.

"Can't you do anything for yourself!" he shouted angrily. "You have your own guards. Use them to secure the sepulchre if you are so worried. My men have enough to do keeping the peace over the next few days. Go away and don't bother me with trivialities."

Caiaphas undeterred, remained calm. "We cannot do that. You know it is Passover and our laws prevent us from travelling and working on the Sabbath. Surely you can spare a small detail of soldiers for guard duty."

Eager to be rid of this troublesome priest, who annoyed him like a fly constantly buzzing round his face, Pilate reluctantly agreed and called the Centurion to carry out the order. He worried that the risk of trouble would not be over until the crowds swelling the city to bursting point dispersed from Jerusalem. Unfortunately that would not be for some days yet. The soldiers had orders to break up any gathering of people numbering more than ten. What he needed was a break away from duty, family, soldiers and especially from that two-faced priest. He sighed as his arm reached out for the flagon of wine.

Nicodemus took to his bed, claiming to be sick. Fearing a hammering on the door, which he was sure would spell his doom, he made rapid plans in his head to get away. He intended to go a long way away and for a long time. Maybe he would go across Arabia and onwards to the lands beyond the mountains. He would make arrangements to join the next caravan and see where it took him. Wishing he could leave today but realising there were things to do in preparation, he determined to depart before the end of the week.

Joseph was also making plans. He had a commission to carry troops back to Ephesus, spices and timber to Rome plus oil and wine to Britannia. There he would fill the hold of his ship with tin and hardwood for the return journey. He would make arrangements to carry Mary and John to their sanctuary in Ephesus. Perhaps not this voyage, it was too soon and as he was carrying Roman soldiers it was too dangerous. Also he had to check the small house was safe and secure. He also had to consider Maryam's situation. Would she, could she undertake a long sea voyage in her condition? What did he know about such things!

There was the possibility of Roman soldiers conducting searches for the disciples. He did not fear a forced entry into his home, which he considered safe. He was far too well known and respected by the authorities for anything to happen but if the unthinkable was to occur, he could always make his escape over the roof tops.

I'm too old for this sort of thing, he thought. I can't wait to get back to sea and breathe in some fresh, clean, salt air.

He was determined to avoid Maryam at this time. She kept giving him quizzical looks. He ensured he was never alone, surrounding himself by his family. He then made his excuses saying he had an urgent business meeting with the Roman quartermaster to finalise some listings. Being Roman he did not care about the Sabbath and for a short time, neither did Joseph.

Nicodemus was also causing Joseph concern. Would he fall apart under the strain of his crime of 'body snatching' as he called it? Would the Centurion deny culpability and knowledge for his part of the operation and let the blame fall on the two of them?

"Too many imponderables," he decided. "What will be, will be." He closed and barred the stout door to his office and slept on the couch.

Maryam had been trying all day to catch Joseph alone so she could ask him about the strange scenes she had witnessed the day before but he kept avoiding her. If she moved towards him he moved away. She wanted to speak privately but he was always surrounded by others. When she had knocked on his office door earlier, she found it empty. He had gone out on business and did not return until late evening, where upon he had barred the door and did not respond to her knocks.

Much of Maryam's day had been spent comforting and consoling Mary, who mourned and grieved for her eldest son. She, Mary, had been torn between pride, that her first born child, Son of God, had fulfilled his destiny without hesitation carrying the sins of the world with him, and sadness that the human, Son of Man, had so cruelly been taken from her. She thought about how she had tutored and encouraged the one and loved and cherished the other. Mary stayed in her room all day, not wanting to see or talk to anyone. She could not bring herself to eat and only drank sips of water but even that seemed tainted. She grew tired of people wanting to speak with her and their offers of condolence. She just wanted to be left alone so she asked John to guard her door and let no one enter except Maryam. Her own daughters were celebrating Passover with their husbands' families and possibly, as yet did not know of their brother's death.

Maryam did her best to console Mary, even though her own heart felt like a lump of stone in her chest. She could hear the subdued chatter of Joseph's family as they went through the motions and rituals of this Passover Sabbath. There was no joy in this house. It was as if they were just passing time. The more raucous noise of the city celebrating floated through the closed shutters into the darkened room but she closed her mind and ignored it.

Holding Mary's frail shoulders, Maryam was conscious of her sobs and felt her tears on her face. She had none of her own. Mara had wept most of the night before, tears of sadness for him and regret when she thought of what their life might have been together. She shed tears for herself when she wondered what her future would hold without him to guide and shelter her. Just as she had thought of him dead and broken on the cross, she too felt lifeless and wished she was dead. Her life seemed pointless and without direction. She realised how much they had all relied on him to hold them together.

No wonder they had all separated, run away, got lost. They were as afraid and grief stricken as she was. She felt a wave of compassion and sympathy sweep over her, regretting she had disparaged them so much.

Something niggled at the back of her mind. She racked her brain to remember something he had told her. She thought back to the day he had run amok in the Temple. He had fled from Jerusalem and come straight to her in the shepherd's hut. Mara felt the heat spread through her body as she remembered their passionate love making and the contented stillness afterwards. His words came back to her now.

"Mara my love, you are the strong one. You have more understanding than all the others. I have told you more than them. Your very name 'Mara' tells me you will be the one to gather them together again, like a shepherd. Bring them back to the fold, my love and help them find the way forward." She had mumbled something and then slept. Had it only been a few days ago?

There was nothing she could do this day but care for his mother. The fact that he had entrusted her with this task helped to lift some of the darkness in her mind. She was not sure how she would go about it, or whether the disciples would accept her words but she knew she had to try, for his sake.

In between her visits to Mary and her efforts to speak with Joseph, Maryam took John aside as he kept vigil outside Mary's door.

"When the Sabbath ends and it is dark outside, I want you to go into the city and find some of the others. Each one will know the whereabouts of the rest. Tell them to come here tomorrow morning early. They are to come in ones and twos and to tell no one else. Our Lord left a message for them which I am to deliver."

John looked at him, wide-eyed. "He left a message with you?" he said almost in disbelief. "Tell me what he said and I will tell them."

"No, John. It has to be me," she replied emphatically, a little unsure of what the message would be but knew she would think of something!

Later in the day when John had slipped out, she returned to Mary's room with some bread, cheese and fruit.

"Eat, Mary," she pressed gently. "We will need our strength for tomorrow."

Mary looked at her with glazed eyes and a puzzled frown. "We have business to attend to. I will collect oils and spices to take care of his body before it decays. We must go very early. I know where he is. We will perform the final rites which is only proper. You must be strong for his sake. If you wish we can make arrangements to take him back to Galilee."

Mary had had no thoughts on this matter, expecting someone else perhaps to take responsibility. However, at the thought of doing something positive for her son, she dried her eyes and ate.

Maryam made no mention of the activities of the previous night.

CHAPTER EIGHTEEN

The Third Day

Maryam did not know how long she had slept, or even if she had slept at all. She drifted in and out of dreams, tossing and turning in her bed. Wrapping herself in a blanket against the night chill, she went to the window and opened the shutters. The air was cool and fresh now that the smell of burning flesh had subsided. The moon was still visible in the heavens, so she knew there were still several hours to go before sun rise.

A sudden movement in the courtyard below attracted her attention but before she could call out, "Who's there?" she recognised the figure of Joseph hurrying to the outer door and disappearing down the street.

Where can he be going at this time of night? she wondered. What business is carried out at dead of night? He is acting very strange lately. Tomorrow I will get answers from him somehow.

Before returning to her bed, Maryam checked the jars and pots of perfumed oils, myrrh and aloes that she would take to the tomb to anoint his body. Maybe decay had already set in but she did not care. She would do this one last act out of love for him.

Sleep would not come, her mind was too active. She rose, washed and dressed herself, wrapped some bread and cheese in a cloth then gently woke Mary. They set out through the still dark streets, lit only here and there by torches which had nearly burnt out but which still clung to the wall brackets, casting flickering shadows on the walls as they passed by. They walked quickly and with purpose. Mary was amazed when she was told what Joseph and Nicodemus had done, especially about the involvement of the Centurion. Suddenly she stood stock still and clutched at Maryam's arm, her face pale in the moonlight.

"If he was buried as you say, how will we move the stone covering the entrance? It will be too heavy for us to manage."

Maryam was stunned. She had not thought of this, however, she would find a way even if it meant finding a gardener or some other workman. It was still dark as the two women arrived at the site, although a rosy glow in the sky indicated the approach of dawn from the east. Instead of the huge stone they expected to see blocking their entrance, they saw a great, gaping, black hole.

"Are you sure this is the right place?" asked Mary hesitantly.

"Certain," Maryam swiftly cast her eyes round and spotted the landmarks she had committed to memory and nodded vigorously. "Positive," she added.

They held each other as they slowly stepped forward with trepidation. As their eyes grew accustomed to the darkness of the cave, they could see nothing inside but the large stone slab on the floor. There was no smell of decaying flesh only a sweet aroma of oil and perfume filled their nostrils. There was no body anywhere. Mary noticed a white cloth at one end of the stone.

"Someone has been here recently. This cloth would have wrapped his head. Where is he? Who has taken him? I don't understand what has happened here."

They were startled by a soft voice addressing them. "Why are you looking for the living amongst the dead?"

Spinning round, they saw the silhouette of a man, dressed in white robes, in the doorway. They were tongue-tied and unable to speak. Both women stared, wide eyed.

"He is not here. Did he not tell you that he would rise again from the dead on the third day? Go and tell the others." The apparition stepped back and disappeared.

The two women recovered quickly from their shock and darted forward to question the man further but there was no sign of anyone having been there. Mary was the first to realise what the man had meant. She hugged Maryam, dancing up and down.

"My son is alive again. Praise Be to God. We must tell everyone that he has risen, just like he said he would."

Ever the cautious one, Maryam restrained her.

"No," she begged, shaking her head. "Go back by all means. Find Peter or John or any of the twelve. Tell them that the tomb is empty and that the body has gone. Make them come and look for themselves. People will not readily believe a woman. You know our law says women cannot give witness. It needs a man's word to break the news. Speak to no one else. I will stay here and look for him. Now, go quickly."

Mary gave the cave one last glance, turned, then hurriedly she retraced her steps to Jerusalem. Her heart was pounding and jumbled thoughts charged through her head. What did it all mean? Where was he? Had he really come back from the dead? Had the Centurion taken him? Would they believe her? What would everyone think, say, or do? It was too much for her understanding.

Left alone, Maryam's eyes filled with tears. She searched the tomb one last time, then left to seek him elsewhere.

She was startled by a voice asking why she was crying. Looking up to where the voice came from, she saw a man standing on a low wall above her. The sun had just risen and its rays shone round him, keeping his face in shadow and temporarily blinding her with its brilliance. Presuming him to be the gardener, she shaded her eyes and replied.

"Someone has taken away my Lord and I don't know where to find him. Sir, if you…"

"Mara don't you know me?"

Immediately her hand flew to her mouth to stifle a cry, her eyes widened and her heart leapt with joy.

"Yeshi? Rabboni? Is it really you?" She scrambled towards him and would have flung her arms round his feet had he not stepped back and stopped her with outstretched hands.

"Do not touch me yet," he warned. "I still stink of the grave and have not yet been with my Father. You are the first one to see me. Do you remember what I said to you?"

Memory flashed through her brain. He had said, 'You are the last and the first'. With this memory came understanding. She had been the last person he had looked at as his body gave up life on the cross and now she was the first one he saw in his new life. She felt very humble and marvelled that he had known this, that she was specially marked out by him.

"Why me Lord?"

He spoke softly, "Why you Mara? Because you are the one I have told things to about God that I have told no one else. You understand me more and love God with all your heart. I love you more than all the others, you are carrying my child. You have the strength and knowledge to speak openly and with truth. Make them listen to you Mara. Tell them to stay in Jerusalem for a few more days until it is safe. I will come to them and again to you. You know where you can find me. Now, go my love and tell my brothers the good news."

Maryam rose to her feet and looked into his eyes. They were no longer dulled with pain and anguish but clear and shining. There were no signs of scars where the thorns had dug into his face. He looked as she remembered him the first time they met in that cave in the wilderness.

The cave, she thought. Of course that is where I will find you. Aloud she promised, "I will do everything you ask of me and more. I will remember this day forever." Maryam set off for Jerusalem with a light heart and a spring in her step.

Peter had arrived at Joseph's house early and had quizzed John about Maryam's message but John could not enlighten him further. They presumed that she still slept in an upper room. Neither had had the opportunity to return to the site of the crucifixion and knew nothing of the burial of the body.

"At least I won't have to meet up with Maryam after today," Peter commented, "and good riddance. Women have no place in our affairs. I will be glad to see the back of that meddlesome she-devil."

His reverie was interrupted by sounds of someone entering the house and was taken aback when John opened the door to Mary who was panting from her exertions. She had a wild look on her face and was gabbling.

"He's gone, come quickly and look. He's gone!"

Thinking her grief had turned her mind John gently took her arm, sat her down to rest and gave her some water. His mouth opened with amazement as she brushed him aside and told them what had taken place already this day. In a garbled fashion she related the burial, the stone being rolled away and the apparition reminding them of the third day. Peter felt inclined to dismiss the ramblings as those of a tormented mother but John reminded him that their master had said he would suffer and die, then rise up on the third day.

"Let us at least go and have a look before we pass judgement. We owe him that much. He said when we remembered things their meaning would become clear."

Mary gave directions to them and the two set off on their quest. John reached the rock cave first, being younger but was too afraid to go inside. Peter brushed him aside and entered the tomb. Inside he saw nothing but the white head cloth which he retrieved and then returned to the sunlight.

"It doesn't prove a thing," he argued. "We cannot be sure that it was him in there in the first place. We only have that woman's word for it and I don't trust her."

Back at the house, other disciples had arrived. They found Maryam and confronted her. Not only was she adamant that their master had indeed been buried in Joseph's family tomb and that the body was no longer there she also claimed to have seen him and spoken with him. There was uproar in the room. Shouts of anger and disbelief mingled with cries of joy and happiness.

"Don't lie to us woman!"

"What did he say?"

"Where was he?"

"How did he look?"

"It is the third day, he is risen up."

"Praise be to God."

"Where is he now?"

Maryam smiled happily as she listened to their excited chatter. She had not expected them to believe her – a mere woman. As they pressed closer round her she held up her arms and they were quiet. She told them of how she had first not recognised him then how he looked.

"He sends a message to you all. He knows you are afraid and grieving. He spoke of his love for all of you and urges you to be strong. He asks that you remain in Jerusalem for a few days more and promises he will come to you himself soon."

Peter was beside himself with anger. "Who do you think you are?" he raged, putting his face close to hers. "Don't you be telling us what to do! Why should we believe anything you say? You are nothing to us!"

As if stung by Peter's harsh words, Matthew came to her defence and stood between them.

"Peter," he growled, "you've never liked Maryam but this is not the time for recriminations. You've always had a quick temper. You know he loved her as much if not more than any of us. Don't be so quick to condemn her or treat her badly." Others nodded their agreement and Peter stepped back.

Maryam was totally unabashed but glanced gratefully at Matthew, then turned back to face Peter.

"Think what you like about me Peter. I'm not afraid of you anymore. Look at me. Look at Mary. Do we seem to be grieving for the loss of a loved one? We are both happy. I tell you he is risen up. I have seen and spoken with him. Do you really think I would make up the story? Why would I lie to you about him? What reason could I possibly have? It is the truth, believe me."

Peter's mouth tightened but he said nothing. Phillip agreed it would be wise to stay in Jerusalem for safety's sake anyway and the others nodded their heads. There was much discussion about what Maryam had told them and they wanted to believe with all their hearts that their master was alive and would return to them. They decided to meet frequently, to gather any news of Roman or Temple retribution, to pray to God and hope that they would see him soon. They left Joseph's house in two's and threes so they would not arouse any suspicions and returned to their hiding places.

Back at Pilate's home the Centurion broke the news of the disappearance of the body of the one they had called The King of The Jews. Pilate blanched and his face visibly whitened. He demanded to know how such a thing could have happened after setting guards to watch and ordering a seal to be placed on the stone. The Centurion reported that the guards had felt an earthquake and had been knocked unconscious but that in his opinion they had fallen asleep on duty. As a punishment he had ordered them to be dispatched to Rome as soon as possible and in the meantime they were confined to barracks and under close arrest. Pilate nodded his agreement.

"The priest will have to be told. He will be furious but what can we do? Tell Caiaphas that the disciples took the man and we will search for them. They have probably fled anyway so rampaging through the streets will only stir up unrest. I will leave it to you as to how 'thorough' the search will be and how long it will last."

Nodding his understanding, the Centurion took his leave and went straight to the High Priest's home with his escort of soldiers. Caiaphas was still recovering from the shock of seeing the Holy of Holies in ruins and the Centurion feared that this latest piece of news would give him apoplexy. Surprisingly, Caiaphas remained calm and thanked the Centurion for coming personally with the information. He said he was grateful that Roman soldiers would search for all the men involved, especially the one who prophesied he would rise again. He agreed to spread the word round the city of a reward for news leading to the arrest of the disciples but did not hold out much hope. The Galileans were a close knit lot.

The Centurion returned to the fortress to make ready for the return journey to his base in Capernaum with his cohort of men. He was utterly sick of Jerusalem and longed for the peace and quiet of the area north of the Sea of Galilee.

Simon and Cleopas had left the city that afternoon to walk back to their home village of Emmaus a distance of about seven miles. They were farmers and had work to do in the fields. They could not waste time idling in Jerusalem. They were earnestly discussing the events of the past week when they were joined by a stranger, his face covered against the dust from the road.

"What is the news?" the stranger asked. It was a customary greeting amongst travellers, as acceptable as commenting on the weather.

"Where have you been this last week?" Cleopas asked incredulously. "Haven't you heard anything about what has been going on in Jerusalem lately?" Cleopas poured out the whole story of the prophet from Galilee, how their own rulers had condemned him to death and how the Romans had crucified him just before Passover. "It is now the third day and rumours are flying that the body has gone, that he is alive again and soldiers are looking for him."

The man sighed and said, "All that you are saying was told many times in the scriptures. They were not just stories but people never really believed these things in their hearts. If they had remembered what Moses, Elijah and even John the Baptist had prophesied they should have realised that the man from Nazareth did in fact fulfil them."

As it was getting late in the day, they invited the stranger to stay with them and eat in their home. The stranger smiled to himself. Just like old times, he thought. He thanked them, removed his sandals and outer garment and sat at the table. Simon placed bread, cheese, dates and water before them. When they saw the man take up the bread, break it into pieces and bless it both men realised who it was at their table. It was the same man who had shared bread with them and thousands of others many months ago on that mountain side. They were rooted to the spot as their Lord and Master smiled, nodded his acknowledgement and took his leave.

Galvanised, they immediately ran out of the house. With no thought of food they set out for Jerusalem as quickly as possible, to the place where they knew he had eaten with his disciples. At first there was no response to their knocking but Simon and Cleopas knew that at least some of the disciples would be hiding inside. They called out softly and eventually they heard the bolt being drawn and the door opened cautiously.

"It is late. Who are you and what do you want?" It was James who spoke.

"We are followers of the Master. We have been baptised," whispered Cleopas.

"We have seen him," added Simon. The door was opened wide and they were welcomed inside. They told their story of meeting the stranger and how he had explained the scriptures in great detail. "But it wasn't until he broke bread and blessed it that we knew who he was," finished Simon. At this final detail the disciples felt their hearts lighten and their pulses race. A babble of excitement broke out. Thanks were given to God for his deliverance then small doubts set in once more. Why was it that he had shown himself to a woman and then to strangers before his most beloved and trusted followers? How could they believe until they had seen him with their own eyes? There was such an intense discussion that they failed to notice a stranger enter the room.

"Peace be unto you, my brothers," the man called out quietly. Silence fell as everyone turned to look at him, their mouths agape as though they were seeing a ghost.

"It is I who stand before you, not a ghost or a spirit. See. I have flesh and bones." He held out his arms for them to touch and they saw the deep holes in his palms where the nails had been. They no longer doubted that he had risen but niggling thoughts of him being human still worried some of them.

"Why did you doubt Maryam? Why didn't you believe Simon and Cleopas? Do you only believe what you see and hear? Do you still have doubts in your minds? I am real. I am alive. I am the same man you knew. I am human – and I'm hungry. Is there any salt fish, it always was my favourite?"

Laughter and tears of joy broke out as they all hugged and embraced one another. They had so many questions but now was not the time. They ate a meagre supper of bread, honey, and fish, not the sumptuous repast of their last meal together but to them, it was the best ever.

When they had finished he took his leave, urging them to stay in Jerusalem a little while longer. He promised he would return and deliver God's message. No one had commented on Judas' absence, but he reminded them that they represented the twelve tribes of Israel, not eleven. Then quietly he said, "Do not think too badly of Judas. He had no choice but to fulfil his destiny as I did mine and as you all must do." He left as quietly as he had come.

Maryam woke with a start. She had been dreaming of a beautiful place somewhere across the sea. Once again she was in a cave but this one was large and airy. It had rugs on the floor and some pieces of furniture which she knew to be hers although she did not recognise them. Outside, a child was playing and she could hear her singing in a strange language that she did not understand. She was about to call out the child's name when she heard her own name spoken and awoke.

There was no one in the room but she felt his presence.

"Yeshi, is that you? Are you here?" she whispered.

"I told you I would be with you always," came the reply. "Mara, there are things that I must do. I have spoken with my brothers and they are like children. They do not yet realise that I cannot be with them as before. It is not possible. My time here is short, only a matter of a few weeks before I must leave them permanently. Then they will be on their own. I will try to make them understand but you must help me. I will send God's spirit to guide them. Once they go their own way they will be better off without me. Make them strong, Mara, give them resolve."

"I do not think they will all listen to me but I will do my best. They do not know about our child Yeshi, so I too must leave, maybe I will go with Joseph somewhere warm where our daughter can grow up safe and sound. None of us can stay here. There is too much danger and hate. Somehow I will convince them. We cannot allow your work to fade away, it must thrive and spread."

He laughed. "Now I know why I love you Mara! You grasp things so quickly. You will achieve our goals. Now sleep well my love. We will speak again and if you need me I will be listening."

Maryam felt his energy leave her space. She sighed contentedly and slept.

CHAPTER NINETEEN

"...Sweet Sorrow"

Maryam knew exactly where to find him. She hastily gathered together some clothing and provisions and sought out Phillip. She told him that she was leaving for a short while but she would return, hopefully with more news of their beloved Master. She joined a caravan of travellers going north from Jerusalem through Judea and Samaria and on to the province of Galilee. Most of the travellers were families who had visited relatives and friends for the Passover celebrations. Their conversations centred mainly round births, marriages and deaths since their last visit. A lot of good humoured gossip passed back and forth to while away the tedium of the journey. Some were on foot, aided by stout walking sticks and carrying small packs on their backs. Others, especially children, rode on carts pulled by oxen, rode donkeys or camels. The more wealthy travellers rode on horseback often escorting fine carriages fitted with cushions and with ornate embellishments. Nearly everyone was carrying gifts, either bought or given to them, for those at home unlucky enough not to have been to Jerusalem because they were too young, too old, infirm or those whose work did not allow them time for holidays.

Other travellers were merchants, their wagons or beasts of burden laden with goods to trade. They carried fine cotton goods from Egypt together with spices such as cinnamon which came by ship from land far across the sea. They traded in woollens, wine, oil, grain, stone, metal and wooden artefacts, anything so that they could make a good living. Alongside them ambled goats and strings of camels to be sold for meat, skins or replenish stocks. These animals stopped at every opportunity to graze the sparse grasses along the roadside and had to be cajoled or driven back into line. Stray dogs followed and trotted between the travellers, hoping to pick up scraps of food along the way.

Between towns and villages, they liked to travel in the early morning or late in the afternoon when it was cool. In the heat of the day they would find shelter from the blazing sun under trees, by watering holes or in the shade of a ravine. By night, they would gather close together, better to protect themselves from bands of marauding robbers or wild animals looking for food. Fires were lit for cooking and gave them light as well as warmth from the chill of the night air.

This was the time to relax, feed the animals and discuss the events of Passover week. The main topic concerned the Nazarene. It seemed everyone had a different story to tell. Some described the joyful entry into Jerusalem on a donkey and how he had averted a confrontation with the Roman soldiers. Another told of his incredible display of anger in the Temple. One had been at the fortress and witnessed the release of Barabbas. Two or three of them had been in the street and watched the wretched man struggling to carry his cross. No one admitted to being at the site of the crucifixion but everyone remembered the strange storm that had plunged the city into darkness not long after midday.

Opinions varied as to the meanings of these strange events. Some, who had met or heard the preaching of the man previously, declared him a Holy man who did not deserve to be put to death, especially by the Romans since Pilate had already found him innocent of any crime. Others declared him as a deranged madman, trying to stir up trouble and bring the wrath of God down on them. One or two told of the rumours that he had risen from the dead and that he had been seen, so maybe there was some truth in the claims of his followers that he was the Son of God. Whatever the truth of the matter was, the happenings made for fine stories to tell when they got back home.

Maryam listened and said nothing – she was a mere woman – what did she know about anything?

The caravan rolled on for days, losing some of their numbers along the way, to Jericho, Ephraim, Arimathaea and on through Samaria. Newcomers joined them and the stories were told and retold along the way. This would be repeated all the way through Palestine, Phoenicia, Syria, Asia Minor and beyond.

Maryam left her companions in Galilee, between the villages of Nain and Nazareth. She clucked and encouraged her donkey, which high-stepped over the sun bleached boulders, up the ever increasingly steep trail to the cave where she found him nearly three years ago.

Upon arrival at the mouth of the cave, Maryam removed her headdress and shook out her hair. Some of the curly tendrils clung to the thin layer of dust and perspiration on her brow. She shook her feet and patted down her clothing to rid them of the dust from the trail and started to unload the food and water from the panniers on the donkey.

"Let me help you with that."

Maryam spun round and her heart filled with joy as she looked into his smiling face. For a moment neither of them moved, drinking in each other's presence. Without saying a word they simultaneously stepped forwards and held each other tightly. There was nothing and no one else in the universe.

They spent the next few days in blissful happiness, not giving a thought to the outside world. Both were content with the present and their togetherness. They were like children, living for the moment, eating, drinking, sleeping, walking, playing and talking. They found it hard to be separated and spent most of their time holding each other's hands, locked in an embrace or making love, unaware of time or place. They slept at odd times and often talked right through the night. He described to her his feelings as he was nailed to the cross.

"I did not feel immune to the pain, after all I was, am, human. I was so afraid. At one stage I didn't think that I would make it up to Calvary, my back stung and my legs felt so weak. I thought that God was testing me one more time. I even hoped that if I could only make it to that awful place, He would somehow relent and save me but it was not to be. I think it was when I saw you face soaked from the rain that I finally knew there was nothing left to hope for."

Maryam cradled him in her arms and comforted him.

"I really thought you had gone, Yeshi, that I would never see you again. I felt very strange at the time. I was angry at the Romans and the Priests. I felt pity for myself, sadness that you had gone, yet happiness that you were no longer feeling pain and suffering. I was very confused and felt a great emptiness at the same time. It is hard to explain but I felt numb and grief-stricken. I certainly had no thought, or idea that we would spend time together again like this. This is heaven on Earth."

"You are right, Mara, The Kingdom of God is just like this, peace, love and happiness in the hearts of men. Those who truly love God will experience this feeling throughout eternity. People, men and women, will find the Kingdom Of Heaven right here in their human lives if they follow my teaching and words. The way to salvation is through me to the individual self of one's own heart. If they lose a loved one, of course they will grieve but they should remember that the lost one will be with God and waiting to be reunited in Heaven. This is why I want my brothers to tell the whole world about me. There will come a time when there are enough believers that the apostles, the interpreters of my words, will no longer be needed. The word of God and my teaching will spread like a huge wave, gathering strength and travelling faster until it covers the whole of the shore, leaving it cleansed and pure."

They sat for a long time, each with their own thoughts. He sat behind her, his arms round her waist and his head cradled on her shoulder. She doodled in the sand at her feet with a small stick. He felt her back stiffen and heard a laugh gurgle from her mouth. He looked over her shoulder to see what had amused her. She had drawn a little shoal of fish in the sand.

"Look Yeshi." she giggled. "These are my fish that you love so much, from Galilee. I will always think of you when I see or eat them." Then she wrote the word 'fish' in the sand. He saw that she had written the word in Greek, 'IXOYS'.

"Can you see it Yeshi? Can you see what I have written?"

"I can see the word 'fish' under the drawings of fish in the manner we teach children."

"Then let me teach you something." She hugged herself with childish excitement. He remembered a game they had played as children, making up silly sentences from a jumble of letters.

"Look at the individual letters. The first is 'Iota' or 'I'. This is the first letter of your name. The second is 'Chi' as in 'Christos', thirdly we have 'Theta' spelling the beginning of the word 'Theos' meaning 'of God' 'Y' could start 'Yios' which is 'Son' and lastly, there is 'Sigma' the Greek letter 's' for 'Soter' translated as 'Saviour'. So, tell me, my love. What does the word 'fish' stand for?"

223

He stood and clapped his hands. "I applaud you Mara. It says 'Iesous, Christos, Theos, Yios, Soter' or, 'Jesus Christ, God's son, Saviour'. What a wonderful way to be remembered – as a fish!" They both hooted with laughter and danced around scattering the sand to the winds with their feet.

Nearly a week had passed but neither seemed aware of the passage of time, so wrapped up were they in each other. Mara wished they could spend the rest of their lives in this barren place, which to her was the most beautiful on God's earth. She sensed however, a withdrawal from her, a darkening of his spirit and knew that their time together was drawing to a close. She did not want him to just disappear from her view, so she decided to be the first one to leave.

"What do you want me to do, Yeshi? Where shall I go?" she asked, one sunny morning.

"Mara, it pains me to part with you. These last few days have been the happiest of my life on earth. I gave up my spirit to become human and now it is close to the time when I must leave again. Go back to Jerusalem, find my brothers and tell them to gather on the Mount of Olives just outside Jerusalem. I will come to them one last time, after which they will see me no more. Tell them all that I have told you and to remember all my teachings. In time they will understand as you do and be strong."

He loaded up her donkey and helped her onto its back. Both had tears of sadness in their eyes. As a parting gesture he stroked her belly and felt a kick to his hand as Sophia stirred into life. He laughed.

"She is punishing me for leaving you to bear this alone." Then he became serious. "You are never alone, Mara. Do not be afraid. I will watch over you, both of you, always."

"Amen," replied Maryam and turned away from him for the last time. There was sadness in her heart but determination in her mind.

The disciples were restless. It had been several weeks since the crucifixion. There had been several 'sightings' of the Nazarene but no further word had come to them. They felt abandoned and directionless. They spent their time reminiscing, praying and discussing the future but could not come up with a workable plan. The Roman soldiers had ceased combing the city looking for them and the Centurion had returned to Capernaum with his troops. Caiaphas, however, had spies everywhere and the disciples rarely ventured out. The city had returned to its normal, everyday way of life. The disciples' womenfolk had returned to their homes in Galilee, with the exception of Mary and her son James. They remained in the house of Joseph of Arimathaea, who was away at sea. On his return they would make preparations to sail to her new home in Ephesus where she would spend the remainder of her days in seclusion and peace.

On one occasion, Phillip brought up the subject of recording the sayings and actions of the master.

"We should write everything down that we can remember, so that we can refer back to it."

Peter, who always shied away from the use of a quill or sharpened reed, shook his head and replied, "There is no need for that. He said the Kingdom of God is coming soon so if Judgement day is at hand, people will know about him first hand."

Phillip argued that people needed knowledge. "Stories can get distorted and word of mouth often veers from the true word. Besides," he continued, "we also need to be clear in our own minds on what has happened, where and when so that what we say is accurate."

One or two agreed with Phillip but the majority came down on the side of Peter, whom they now regarded as their leader. Most of them could not write anyway and relied on their own memories, experiences and their ability to heal.

Phillip, with Nathanial had made copious notes throughout their time with the Master and continued to write to while away the long hours spent waiting for his return. John also wrote his account of the mission they had all undertaken. He felt he owed it to his beloved Lord because he had been singled out as a favourite disciple and wanted to be remembered as such.

As more and more days of inactivity went by, the disciples felt ever increasing frustration at their idleness. They all thought that they should be doing something, anything would be better than this waiting game. They were reluctant to disperse and return to their former lives as some had suggested. To do so would render their work over the last few years as pointless. Some suggested that their mission had been completed anyway. The majority were persuaded that they must resist the temptation to give up and to remain as they were for the foreseeable future as he had told them. Nerves were beginning to fray and sometimes arguments broke out, usually over the most trivial things, but they could not seem to help themselves.

It was during one of these sessions of petty bickering that Maryam arrived at the house. She had first called upon Mary, to pay her respects and report that her son was well and happy, sending her his love. Knowing that Mary would soon be leaving the country, she bade her farewell but first confided that she would become a grandmother in the not too distant future. Mary smiled happily at this information, which she already suspected and urged Maryam to somehow find a way to let her see her grandchild at some time in the future.

When she entered the upper room where the disciples were incarcerated, Phillip and Matthew jumped up to embrace her. Nathanial waved and gave her a welcoming smile. James ignored her while Peter scowled and rolled his eyes. Soon the others surrounded her, begging for news when they heard she had come from him in the wilderness. She was as eager to tell them as they were to listen.

"First, he sends his love to all of you and thanks you for not losing faith in him. He said that he will send God's spirit to guide you and whatever the spirit tells you, you know that it comes from him.

"In a few days' time you must go to the Mount of Olives, where he will come to you for the very last time. Then he will go to his Father and prepare places for all of you. He says you know the way."

"How can we know the way?" interrupted Thomas, "when we have never been there."

"He says he is the way and that you must follow him." Looking directly at Peter, Maryam continued. "You must believe what I am telling you because he says I am to him what Sheba was to Solomon." Peter screwed up his eyes but did not comment as he too wanted to know more. In his heart he knew that what the Migdahl woman said was the truth.

"Furthermore, he asks that you remember everything he said and did and teach in his name. If you need something, or want to do something, all you have to do is ask for it in his name and he will grant your wish. He will help you to know who you are. Remember, like him you are only human and will make mistakes. To follow him is to be truly human. We are all accountable to God for our life on this earth, so praise His greatness. His greatest gift to us is his love. We must love ourselves, each other and God with great passion. This is his message, his legacy from his time on earth."

There were many questions asked and answered. The disciples talked animatedly well into the night.

"Did he say what heaven is like?"

"It is like peace and joy in our own hearts."

"Should we teach the Gentiles?"

"If they will listen."

"Should we build a monument?"

"The individual is his monument."

"What if we are persecuted?"

"He will protect you."

"What about sacrifice?"

"Only that you should be willing to lay down your own life for others and your faith."

"When is God's kingdom coming?"

"It is God's decision, not ours to know."

"Are we to be like priests?"

"No priests. Just the individual and God."

The conversation flowed, even Peter became involved but could not help asking "What did he say about preaching to women?"

"He said, 'forget gender, think instead individual or best of all human being'." With that Maryam winked and Peter grinned, saluting her by touching his fingers to his forehead. At long last they had reached a truce!

There was so much to talk about their boredom and animosity disappeared in a twinkling. They were almost too excited to sleep but one by one they dozed where they sat or lay, each dreaming of the time they would see him again. Maryam huddled in a corner at the far end of the room, content that they had accepted her words, even Peter.

"Yeshi," she called silently. "You have done it again. It is you and your words that bring this disparate group of people together and mould them into a force to be reckoned with."

"My words, your voice, Mara. For which I thank you. Your work here is done except for one last thing. Go back to my mother and prepare to leave this place with her. Whether you stay with her or travel further is your choice. Whilst you are waiting for Jofa, talk to my brother James. He is still a devout Jew and follows the laws of Moses but he has enough knowledge and understanding of my ministry to adapt his teaching. Tell him I would like him to stay in Jerusalem and with the help of other converts like Nicodemus and Jofa to set up a group of followers in my name. The others are not safe in Jerusalem. They will be hounded but I have no such fears for James. Now sleep, my love. I will come to you in your dreams, in your mind and always in your heart."

Maryam sighed, content with her achievements. She did not know where she would go but would wait and see where the winds and Joseph's sails took her.

CHAPTER TWENTY

The Final Days

Each day the eleven faithful men set out for The Mount of Olives, not far from Gethsemane, where on that fateful night the Master had been taken from them. They waited from early morning until dusk, eating little but spending their time in prayer and private contemplation. Gone was the boredom and the bickering, replaced by anticipation of his reappearance and uncertainty as to what the future might hold for them.

They were no longer afraid of retribution by the Roman soldiers in Jerusalem but had heard that Caiaphas had recruited a man named Saul to hunt them down. Saul was Jewish by birth but had been born in Rome itself, giving him a certain status as a Roman citizen. His family had left Rome and now lived in Tarsus. Like many other Jews who lived outside Israel, Saul had made his pilgrimage to the city of David for the Passover and had remained there. He had been welcomed by the Sadducees because of his wealth and standing and also by the Temple elders because of his unerring devotion to the laws of Moses, plus substantial gifts to the coffers. Whereas he had no prior knowledge of the Nazarene, of whom there had been so much talk lately, he considered anyone who set themselves up in opposition to the priesthood and claimed to be 'King of The Jews' was an abomination and deserved to be wiped off the face of the earth.

On the fifth day the wait was over. As they sat in the cool shade of the olive trees, they were aware that he sat with them but no one had seen him approach. Knowing their fears for the future and of persecution in particular, he reassured them saying,

"Do not doubt yourselves. I will protect you and God will guide you." They sat close to him for a while asking him questions but mainly content just to be near him. He told them to go to the ends of the earth. "Feed my sheep." To Peter he said, "Be the shepherd," and to Thomas, "Blessed are those who have not seen me but still believe."

At last he rose and went a little way up the hillside so that he could address them all.

"It is time for me to leave you. There is so much more for you to learn and understand. All will become clear in a few days. I will send the Holy Spirit to counsel you. As my Father sent me, so do I send you. Whatever you say or do, do it in my name. You will not see me again in this life. You will be stronger without me, so it is for your benefit that I am leaving. Be happy for me that I am returning to my Father. Remember all that I have told you and that I love you always."

As he stood above them the last few rays of the evening sun shone around him, seeming to radiate from his body straight into their eyes and they were temporarily blinded. After blinking and rubbing their eyes several times, they looked to where he had stood but there was nothing except the sighing of the wind as it rippled through the trees. No one expressed surprise or amazement, each accepted that he had gone and would not be returning. They knelt together for a short time and prayed to God, thanking Him for the privilege of knowing His son. Once more they returned to the upper room in Jerusalem feeling that the bond between them and the Master would last forever. They were glad that the weeks of waiting were nearly over and they could begin the tasks he had set them.

Their first task was to make up their number to the original twelve as he had reminded them. Many times they had thought of who should replace the one who had betrayed their Lord. They could hardly bring themselves to speak his name. Apparently, all the plants in the field where he had hanged himself had withered and died. Nothing grew there now, so the tainted Temple coins, which were found below his body, were used to buy the ground which would then be used to bury bodies that were not claimed by families or friends and would subsequently be called The Field of Blood.

They considered the members of the original seventy or so followers from whom they themselves had been chosen. They too had gone out into the countryside, towns and villages, telling people about the rabbi and exhorting them to repent of their sins become baptised and follow him. They had given food and shelter to the twelve and had kept the faith throughout his ministry. Some were better known to the disciples than others but there was no obvious successor to become the twelfth man they knew they must choose.

Eventually they whittled the numbers down to two but after much discussion they still could not decide. The two were Joseph Barsabbas, known as Justus, and Matthias. It was Peter's suggestion that they let God decide. Each disciple prayed earnestly for guidance to choose the correct one, then they drew lots and the honour was given to Matthias. They welcomed him as a brother and now felt ready to do the Lord's work.

Ten days after the Master had left them the newly formed twelve went to the Temple to celebrate God's gift of the ten Commandments to Moses, fifty days after his exodus from

Egypt and the same number of days since the crucifixion. The day was called Shavuot or Pentecost. They knew that they risked the wrath of the Temple priests, so did not enter the Temple itself but stayed in the safety of the crowds which gathered on the steps of Solomon's Portico. Mary and her other sons were with them.

As they stood there close together a sudden, strong, driving wind sprang up and roared across the courtyard, forcing them to gather their clothing tightly round them. Blinding shafts of sunlight caught them appearing to surround their heads in fire. They felt a great pressure on them and gripped their hands to their ears as a thousand thoughts and images flashed through their minds. Just as quickly as it had come, the wind ceased and the disciples breathed easily.

They all spoke at once, expressing their wonder and amazement at what had just occurred.

"What was that?"

"What just happened?"

"Did you feel it?"

"I thought I would die."

"My head felt as if it would burst."

"Thank goodness that is over."

"It was wonderful."

"Everything seems so clear now."

"What does it mean?"

Since they stood at the Temple, a focal point for Jews from many countries, they were surrounded by many visiting people each with their own language. They saw what had happened and heard the group of men speaking. Each one heard the words in his own language and was amazed. Everyone understood that something very strange and wonderful had happened to these Galilean Jews.

Realisation dawned on the twelve that they had just been given the spirit of God as promised and the time had come for them to begin their own ministries. Peter, all fired up with zeal took the opportunity to openly tell all those around him about the words and works of the Nazarene, the Son of God, his life, death and resurrection. Many were converted that day.

Caiaphas had them brought before him and interrogated. He saw that they were only rough rural laymen and did not constitute much of a threat. He would have liked to imprison them but because there was such a fervour round the Temple he refrained from punishing them. Instead he ordered them not to speak in public about this resurrection nonsense and discharged them.

The twelve were no longer pupils but interpreters of their master's teachings and therefore were apostles, not disciples any more. They left Jerusalem and returned to Galilee, preaching with a new clarity as they went. They had a deeper understanding of the ancient prophesies and how they had been fulfilled. All of them were eager to go out into the world and spread the word.

After a few days together praying, sorting out their affairs, preparing for their journeys and saying farewell to their families, the apostles set off on their travels. They split into small groups which would subdivide along the way and headed in different directions. One group went south to Egypt, Sinai and Libya. Another crossed the River Jordan into Arabia. A third went to Babylon in Mesopotamia and even beyond. The largest number travelled north, through Syria, into Cappadocia splitting up to cover Asia Minor and onwards to Thrace and Macedonia. One or two sailed with Joseph spreading their message to the islands of the Mediterranean. John sailed with Joseph from Caesarea to Ephesus with Mary as he promised. He set up a small school there knowing that the children would accept and believe his words.

Everywhere they all went they urged people to be baptised and to pass on the message given to them by the Son of God, the anointed one. Their teaching caused ripples which spread throughout the lands by word of mouth and by example. The life of their Master may have ended but his ministry had just begun.

Epilogue

The bustling port of Tyre was a second home to Joseph. He had been brought here by his own father as a boy of ten years. He loved every cubit of it. The salt breezes from the sea had refreshed his senses far more than the dry, stifling air of Arimathaea. It was not as modern as the port of Caesarea Maritima, built by old King Herod, but it was more welcoming.

He knew it well, from the streets and market place of the old town down to the warehouses crammed up against each other along the waterfront, jostling for space. All kinds of goods were stored and traded here, salt for tin or lead, wine and oil for gold and spices, grain for hardwood, woollen cloth and carpets for trinkets or furnishings, hunting dogs, falcons, farm animals, even slaves were bought and sold in the open air auctions.

Taverns and brothels were always busy and there was an energy to the port that Joseph found exhilarating, like nowhere else. He had his own storage place carefully guarded by his men against robbers and pilferers. Like all the other traders, he bought and sold, took and delivered special orders and commissions, bargained hard but was always fair. He had earned a reputation of being honest and trustworthy.

Joseph was proud of his ships. He had expanded their number from his father's day to form a small fleet. Some were small and narrow, not as large as the Roman triremes, but built for speed with tall curving prows and one steering oar at the stern. Others were broader with a shallow draught used for transporting heavy cargoes of grain, timber, oils, wine and anything else he could stow on board. All his vessels had tall masts, strong sails and doughty oars. Often several ships set sail together for protection against rogue pirate ships or to rescue men and goods from any ship unfortunate enough to be blown off course onto rocks or damaged by storms.

One fine evening, Joseph made his way down to his ship in the harbour. He eagerly inhaled the intermingled smells of spices, animals and the acrid smell of black, sticky, pitch used to caulk the ship's timbers. He cast an expert eye over the remaining bales of wool still to be loaded. He heard the good humoured shouts of the shore men as they struggled to carry the goods up the flimsy, wavering gangplank. On board sailors of many different origins were checking ropes holding the furled sails in place slapping against the mast. He could see them running along the decks, hurrying to complete their tasks before the sun set and thinking of spending a few hours in the tavern before sailing at first light. Their first port of call would be north to Patara in Asia Minor, so were hoping for a fair wind. Oars were secured and resting quietly against their stocks, well- oiled and ready to do battle with the waves to the steady beat of the drum.

The oarsmen with sturdy backs, strong arms and legs were from many different sources. Some had been Roman slaves whose freedom had been bought. Others were rogues and vagabonds who preferred a life at sea to one in prison. Yet more were old salts who loved the adventure of voyages and made an honest living by their own sweat.

Joseph took pleasure in all he heard and saw. He had said his farewells to his family and friends as he had done many times before. Humming to himself, he checked the cargo, galley, mast and sails then spoke with his loyal captain of many years. Having been assured that all was well and shipshape, he prepared to turn in for the night. He was looking forward to sleeping in his bunk, rocked by the gentle rolling swell of the sea and lulled to sleep by the soft lapping of the waves against the ship's hull.

He climbed down the steps to his cabin below decks and cast a cursory glance round his small space. It was sparsely furnished; a small narrow cot, a cupboard for his few belongings, a table securely fastened to the wall with navigation charts, scrolls of parchment and lists of buyers matched with cargoes. There were two chairs; one padded the other a plain rustic wood. A couple of sturdy jars stood on the floor one filled with wine and the other with water.

Joseph looked tired as he surveyed this small centre of his empire, this little haven of peace. It had been a stressful few months and the strain was etched on his weather-beaten face. He sighed as he trailed his hand along the table. It had been made especially for him at the carpenter's shop in Nazareth by another Joseph, now long gone, as a 'thank you' gift for taking his son on his voyages many years before.

He slumped into his chair and reached for a flagon to pour himself a little wine. Startled by a small movement in the darkest corner of the cabin, he jumped to his feet. A man, dressed in the striped robes of a merchant, eased himself up from the narrow bunk.

"Who are you? What are you doing here?" demanded Joseph, his heart suddenly beating fast. "We have no room for passengers on this voyage." He backed away, overturning his chair and afraid that the man meant him harm. He prepared to call for the captain to throw the interloper off the ship.

"Wait," ordered the merchant harshly and then more softly he said, "we had an agreement to meet here. Don't you remember?"

Joseph stumbled as though his legs would give way underneath him. He clutched the table for support, his face paled under his tan. Neither man spoke for a few minutes and then Joseph tentatively reached forward for a flint to light the wick of an oil lamp. At first the flame sputtered, throwing flickering shadows that danced across the walls of his cabin before settling down to a steady glow, illuminating the man's features.

It was difficult to tell the man's age. His face was covered by a thick, bushy beard and his forehead hidden by the hood of his burnoose. Dark eyebrows shaded his eyes until he raised his head slightly. The light of the lamp caught deep brown pools, flecked with gold which seemed to bore right through him. It was as if they were compelling Joseph to remember him. They burned into him, staring and unblinking. There was no further doubt in his mind. Joseph's heart and soul were filled with joy and happiness. A huge smile lit his face as he spread out his arms wide and leapt forward to greet his visitor. Tears flowed unhindered down his lined cheeks as they hugged, laughed and jiggled round the small cabin, reluctant to let each other go.

Eventually, exhausted by their emotions, both men collapsed into chairs and wiped away tears of joy with their sleeves. Their faces were beaming and they could not take their eyes off each other.

"Well," gasped Joseph at last. "I think this calls for a drink – a good big hefty one!"

He reached for the flagon of his best sweet wine from Martha's vineyard, which he kept for his own personal consumption. He poured two very generous measures into silver cups.

"Of course I remember you saying that you would meet me here, but you never said when and to be honest…" His voice trembled slightly, "I never thought you would make it. I have not heard any rumours as to where you might be. I haven't dared ask anyone, of course, but I thought one of the others might drop a hint. Not a word though. Where have you been? We have got a lot of catching up to do."

The 'merchant' took a long draught of wine, sighed deeply and settled back comfortably in his chair. He rested his feet on the low padded stool and Joseph caught a glimpse of a dark puckered scar on his ankles. Joseph winced at the memory of that fateful day and surreptitiously checked to match the scars on his hands.

"Oh, I have been here and there, everywhere in fact," he said airily. "I've kept an eye on my brothers. They seem to be coping well and growing in strength and confidence, as I knew they would, without me to rely on. Some have even been arrested and imprisoned temporarily and have survived the ordeal.

But I'm tired, Jofa, tired of wandering, being in disguise, hiding in caves. I'm sick of being scared of discovery and being so alone. I cannot preach openly in case I am recognised and I still have so much more to give. Maybe it would have been better if I had stayed in that dark place and not come back."

There was a silence as the two men turned their thoughts back to the day on Golgotha.

"What happened in there?" asked Joseph, solemnly. "We did everything we could for you but without much hope as you seemed so lifeless when we took you down."

"Not quite lifeless. I was suspended between life and death. There was a darkness in my mind and I felt my soul slipping away. I felt it drift away from my body and hover above me as if it was unsure whether to go or to stay. It seemed to be waiting for my permission to leave. After what felt like an eternity, a pinprick of light appeared above me. This must have been some sort of signal because my soul was galvanised into flight. It ascended towards the light and took my consciousness with it. The roof of the tomb opened and we soared through. Instead of seeing the stars and sky, we were in some sort of a tunnel leading ever upwards. The source of light grew in size and brilliance as we came nearer until it was as large as the entrance to a cave.

My soul hesitated at the entrance and I could see heaven itself all around me. It was so light, beautiful and welcoming. There were so many people, all smiling and holding out their arms to me. I recognised most of them, my earthly father, Joseph, my ancestors, even Solomon and King David.

A voice inside my mind whispered, "Are you staying or are you going back?"

It was an easy choice for me. I could go forward to a life of eternal peace and happiness, or return to a life of persecution and torment. I eagerly stepped into the light and welcomed its warmth. Immediately, I stood before God, my Father, with Abraham, Isaac, Elijah, Moses and all the other Prophets nearby. I would have fallen on my knees before Him but He raised me up to sit with Him.

"My Son," He said. "You have done well. We are all so proud of you. You did not falter in your mission or in your sacrifice. I so wanted to relieve you of your burden. I grieved at your pain and humiliation. No one has ever given more than you in My name. Your work on Earth has now finished. Others will carry the word and spread your ministry. That was your gift to Me, now here is My gift to you. I am sending you back to Earth to resume your human form. You will live the rest of your natural life as other men, wherever and however you wish."

All the Prophets embraced me with tears in their eyes. They wished me well, until such time that I would return to them. My Father breathed life into my mouth as though I was a new born child. I began to hurtle down the tunnel until I was back in the tomb."

He paused to drink some of the wine. Joseph did not know what to do or say to the man opposite him. Awkwardly he pushed a copper plate emblazoned with the Star of David, across the table. It was filled with sweet, red grapes, fresh purple figs, dried dates, honeyed walnuts, olives and small biscuits. With a hand he gestured his visitor to eat.

"So, you really did die after all and the Prophesies were fulfilled," he said thoughtfully. "I often wondered if by helping you we had, somehow cheated God and would be punished. Please, go on with your account. I want to know everything."

The man smiled and nodded his head. "Yes," he conceded "I can honestly say I died that day, taking the sins of mankind with me. I would have willingly remained so had it not been for God's intervention.

Anyway," he continued, "back in the tomb, I felt the thud of my heart beat starting up again and my life's blood began to flow from my legs upwards until every part of my body felt it's warmth as I lay in the dark. I was afraid to open my eyes as I was not quite sure where I was. It was too dark to be heaven and too cold to be hell. I didn't know if I was still on the cross, in the tunnel or the tomb. My mind was so confused. If you had not been successful in your efforts I would have died again in the tomb anyway from starvation. I admit I panicked a bit.

However, I eventually calmed down and cracked my eyelids open just a fraction. Instead of total darkness I saw the steady light of the lamp you had left me. I could smell the oils and spices, at first sharp and acrid which helped to clear my head, then after a while they were warm and fragrant. I slowly stretched, testing my muscles and gradually sat up, removing the binding cloths. My feet hands and sides throbbed but no bones were broken and the salve you applied had started the healing process, closing the wounds which had scabbed over.

I was so thirsty I drank the water greedily and ate some of the bread and dates. I felt exhausted and slept a deep healing, refreshing sleep. I do not know how long I slept for, minutes, hours or for over a day. The oil in the lamp was low when I awoke. I found the old clothes you had left for me and had just finished dressing when I heard the grinding of the stone being rolled back and wedged. Unsure if it was you, the Roman soldiers or even the Temple guards. I extinguished the lamp and hid in the darkest recess of the cave. Pale ribbons of grey light filtered through the gloom, clouded by the dust of the stone. I drank in the pure, fresh air, breathing as though for the first time.

Cautiously, I ventured outside. It was not yet dawn but I did not want to be seen so I hid behind a boulder. I saw the Centurion kick the soldiers awake and march them off back to the fortress. I heard voices and saw my mother and Maryam go into the tomb. Then I heard them shout and rush out again. Mother was dancing up and down and ran off, presumably to tell the others that I had risen from the dead. Maryam stayed behind and I called to her. No wonder she did not recognise me in those clothes. Also the sun was behind me, but when I called her name her face was a delight to behold.

She would have flung herself at me had I not stopped her. It was not the right time. We both had things to do. I told her to persuade the brothers to stay in Jerusalem until I was ready to come to them.

The rest you know I think. So now Jofa, it is your turn. How did you manage to take me from the cross after only a few hours? The Romans must have known it takes longer than that to die."

Joseph stood and paced round his small cabin. His mind was reeling from what he had just heard. He had kept his secret for months and at last he felt able to unburden himself of a story he had not told a living soul. He re-seated himself, took a deep breath and began his tale.

"As you are aware, I have a lot of knowledge of and investments in mining. So much that I am an advisor to the Romans on mining exploration. I report to the Governor frequently on new finds or developments. Because of this I have access to Pilate himself in his palace without being questioned by the guards, so getting in to see him was the easy part. I was there that morning, saw and heard everything. Do you remember how reluctant he was to judge you at his so-called 'trials'? I wondered about that, I mean, what did he care? He had found so many others guilty and crucified without blinking an eye. He did not know you and yet he was disturbed, agitated and he even publicly washed his hands of the whole affair.

Well, as they led you away, I saw Pilate's wife, Procula, come out from behind a column. She too had been listening to everything and was very distressed. She beckoned me over and whispered, conspiratorially, that Pilate really did not want you to be put to death. She had had a dream and warned him that if he sentenced you to death and was responsible for your crucifixion, the future held dire consequences for him and his family. He would be stripped of office and returned to Rome in ignominy. Somehow the Galilean must live. She begged me to find a way to rescue you but at the same time to let her husband keep face.

"He will agree to anything almost, if it does not directly involve him," she said.

Joseph paused to catch his breath and marshal his thoughts. He began again.

"I had very little time and no idea what to do. As you waited in the fortress courtyard, I saw the Centurion in charge that day. It was the same one whose servant you healed without even seeing him. I spoke to him urgently saying, 'Is there a way to save him? You know who he is and you owe him. Can you get him down quickly and we will do the rest'.

"He just stared at me and I could see a hundred emotions going across his face. His expression changed and he nodded imperceptibly.

"Leave it with me," he whispered. "Just ask Pilate if you can have the body for burial and I will see what can be done." Then the Centurion strode off purposefully. He picked up a lash and soaked it in a vat of salt water used for cleaning injured horses' wounds. This he gave to the soldier assigned to flog you, saying quietly, "Not too many and not too hard." The soldier was apparently used to administering the lash in varying degrees, so he did as ordered. Because of the salt there was not too much blood from the broken skin. I bet it stung though."

"I remember the lash," the man said, "and the crown of thorns. Those filthy spikes caused more pain than the lash. I remember being mocked and spat upon. Every single staggering step to Golgotha is etched on my mind. I was saddened by the way the crowd of people laughed at my efforts, the same ones who had shouted 'Hosanna' only days before. There was one kind man who helped carry my burden for a short while and a woman who gave me a drink spiked with myrrh to deaden the pain. Every moment of that awful, wonderful day is burned into my memory.

I kept thinking, 'This is it, this is where it all ends' even though I had said to you earlier, 'if there is a way, I will meet you at the port of Tyre'.

I used all my powers of concentration to try to ignore or blot out the pain. I kept praying to my Father, hoping that somehow He might relent and save me but then everything I had done, said, worked for would have been in vain. I realised I had to see it through to the bitter end. I was apprehensive but happy in the knowledge I would soon be with my Father for all eternity.

Only when I was up there, tied, nailed, bleeding and in pain did I lose concentration for a little while. To my shame I cried out loud to ask my Father why He had forsaken me. Towards the end I looked up and saw my mother, John and Maryam. It was getting dark and rain had started when I raised my head and spoke to them one last time. Finally I closed my eyes and mind and went into deep meditation, deeper than anything ever before. I was in a state of relaxation and trance, a practice I had learned many years before. Repeating my mantra, 'Aum' meaning 'I am' I entered into complete forgetfulness and emptiness.

My work here in Israel and on Earth was finished, so I yielded up my body to the darkness. My heartbeat slowed and my breathing was so shallow it would appear as though my body was lifeless. Even my blood flow slowed and settled heavily in my legs. From that point on I remember nothing until I felt my soul slipping away as I told you. Now, tell me Jofa what exactly happened when that strange storm broke?"

Joseph had listened enthralled. His heart was heavy with sadness as he too remembered the pain, the grief and the agony of those terrible hours. He could still see the tears of the women, the cruelty of the soldiers mocking him and throwing dice for his robe. He had had nightmares where he lived the scene over and over, hearing the cracking of bones as they broke the legs of the victims on either side of his beloved Master. He also saw the fear on those malevolent faces as the sky darkened and the terrible storm rocked the earth. He stood, stretched his limbs, shook his head to clear his mind and continued his part in the affair.

"I went back to see Pilate. Again, no one challenged me. He was stretched out on a couch, half asleep, or half drunk, possibly both. He must have thought I was there on business because he asked me how the new tin mine in Britannia was coming along. I mumbled something about potential profits and then said I had come on another matter, to ask a favour of him. He groaned and eyed me suspiciously. He said the last time he had a meeting with the Jews it had ended in a crucifixion. He was not inclined to do any favours.

I persevered and asked if I could have your body as you were a relative and that I would be using my own family tomb. It was only a temporary measure as your mother and brothers would probably want to give you a proper burial in Galilee after Passover had finished. I wanted official permission so that no one could accuse me or your friends of stealing the body to fulfil the Prophesy.

He was very reluctant at first, as it had only been a few hours since he had sent you up there. He would not give permission. I began to panic and pleaded with him. He agreed to send for the Centurion in charge who, unbeknown to Pilate, was waiting in the courtyard for just such a call. The Governor was clearly distressed and said,

'I did all I could. Perhaps I should have ignored Caiaphas but the Priest insisted, saying I was no friend to Tiberius if I allowed the man to go free. I had no answer to this and wishing for neither the wrath of Caesar nor a riot in the city, I washed my hands of the whole affair and just let it happen. My mind is very disturbed over this and I do not think I will sleep well tonight, knowing that I could have stopped it'.

I just shook my head and told him that it was your destiny and that he was merely a player who made the Prophesy happen.

The Centurion entered, drenched by the rain and spattered with mud, flanked by his soldiers. "I came as quickly as I could, Sir. All three are now dead."

Pilate needed reassurance that the so-called 'King of the Jews' was really dead after so little time on the cross. The

Centurion replied, 'Yes' very emphatically. 'His lips were blue. There was no heartbeat, no breathing and only a little blood oozed out when I pierced his side with my sword, only watery fluid. I think he died quickly of heart failure due to all the pain and stress. The other two are also dead but we had to break their legs to finish them off, so they too died quickly.'

Pilate was still not too happy, so I told him that the Sabbath was fast approaching. Our laws prohibited bodies to be left in the open at this time, especially at Passover time. He should be buried straight away or the Jews would be offended, no matter what the crime had been or however much he deserved his punishment. Not wanting to stir up any more trouble, religious or otherwise, Pilate grudgingly gave his consent but stipulated that the Centurion would accompany me as a witness.

As we were leaving, I again saw Procula. She had been listening to everything as usual. She nodded her acknowledgement of the Centurion and I'm sure she gave me a wink! Strange beings, these Roman women!"

Joseph lit the fuels of a shisha water pipe and offered it to his companion, who politely refused saying he had never acquired the habit.

"Anyway," he continued, sucking in the fragrant, cool fruity flavour contentedly. "It was getting late and Nicodemus was fretting outside like a mother hen. He was sure we would be pounced upon at any minute. We hurried to the crucifixion site with the Centurion and the handcart and took you down as carefully as we could. Nobody saw us. Your brothers were in hiding from the soldiers and priests' men. The womenfolk who stayed the longest had gone back to my house in Jerusalem and were mourning. They were too sick to eat or talk to anyone.

We managed to transport your corpse – er, sorry, your body to my family tomb. We dried the mud and rain from the storm from you then oiled and massaged your limbs from head to toe to try to restore your blood circulation. Nicodemus covered your wounds with healing salve including that special one you made up for us with the herbs, myrrh, aloes and crushed mandrake root. We spread the powdered mould from the rotten oranges on the wound in your side, just as you instructed us. Nicodemus, old woman that he is, did a really good job considering the task is usually carried out by women. I just wrapped the linen cloth round you with a few more herbs and spices.

When we had finished we left some old workman's clothes, some food and water and filled up the oil in the lamp. We left quickly and rolled the stone in place to cover the entrance, so that no wild animals could sneak inside. We also made sure the lever was in place to reverse the angle of the channel on which the stone rested so we could easily re-open the tomb after the Sabbath when it was safe. Nicodemus was nearly peeing himself so we left in a hurry.

The Centurion had to set a rota of guards because Pilate had ordered it to be sealed. We had to get home to the families and guests to celebrate the Sabbath and Passover, although 'celebrate' was the wrong word. Nothing was further from our minds.

I don't think anyone slept a wink that night. Everybody was so shocked and distraught at how quickly events had taken place that day. Not one of our people went to the synagogue or Temple on the Sabbath day. We were all either, grieving, ashamed or sickened and didn't want to listen to the ranting of the Temple priests, so we stayed home quietly with the family in prayer or private contemplation.

For some reason Maryam kept trying to get my attention. I'm sure she did not know anything, but I avoided her anyway.

There was a strange atmosphere in Jerusalem that day, I can tell you. It was rumoured that Caiaphas had a heart attack in the Holy of Holies. I think he was struck down by God for all his evil doings. He is still trying to stamp out your influence but without much success.

When the Sabbath had finished, the sun had long since set and everyone had settled down for the night, I called upon Nicodemus and we went secretly back to the garden of the dead to watch over the tomb. There were guards so we couldn't do anything. We just hid and watched them. They changed their watch several times until the early hours of the morning. We thought we would never get a chance to open the tomb but then we saw the Centurion come to check on them. He passed a few words, had a laugh and a joke with them then gave them a drop of something, 'to keep out the cold', he said. It probably would have been date spirit laced with the juice of crushed poppy seeds, because they finally succumbed to sleep.

We only had a short time left to move the stone from the entrance, before they woke or the sun came up, so we did not stay to enter or wait until you came out. To be honest we were scared stiff that we would be discovered and we feared that you were dead anyway, despite our feeble efforts. So I'm sorry to say it but we ran away. Nicodemus and I agreed to say nothing to anyone and try to pretend it never happened. We went our separate ways. I went to my ship preparing to sail to Rome. Nicodemus hastily planned a trading contract and joined a caravan going north. I believe he is back in Jerusalem now and is in touch with your brother James.

As you saw, the Centurion came back and feigned anger at the guards for falling asleep on duty. I believe he sent them away very rapidly back to Rome or Gaul as a punishment for dereliction of duty but really it was just to get them out of the way.

He sent me a message. It simply said,

"I have paid my debt," signed with a crude fish motif. He went back to Capernaum for a short while before returning to

Rome. I heard he had retired and now lives in Tuscany with his family. A good man.

I can only assume that you know the rest of the story. Your mother is settled and happy in her new home. John is still with her and is making many converts. I think he will leave soon to travel with his brother but he will keep an eye on her. Peter has been arrested a couple of times but seems unperturbed. He is working harder than anyone to make amends for denying he knew you.

I was going to take Maryam to Britannia but when we reached the island of Malta she was too close to her time. I thought Britannia would be too cold and inhospitable for her so I detoured the ship to southern Gaul where she disembarked with her friend Salome. I think Phillip is going to join her for a while before going back to Egypt. Anyway, the locals, many of them are Jewish, seemed to take to her immediately and now she is living in a large cave not too far from the port. She is preaching also, mainly to women who are very receptive. She was delivered of a daughter and named her Sophia.

The rest of your brothers, the apostles, are scattered far and wide as you told them spreading your teaching and God's Kingdom. For them, you more than fulfilled the Prophesies. You taught them about love, peace and being human as the way to God. Jewish people never thought about religion in that way.

So, is this the end of it Jeshua? What will you do now? Come with me and we will travel the world spreading the message far and wide. We sail at dawn. What do you say?"

Joseph slapped his thighs at the thought of this new adventure. He would have a new companion in his old age, an heir to his fleet who was a relative, a friend, his Master, Lord and Messiah. He was more than content.

"Maybe, Jofa," Jeshua said, thoughtfully. "Who knows? I would like to be with Mara and my daughter who will one day carry on my work as well as my bloodline. I send my thoughts to Mara in her dreams and I know that she is well and happy. I cannot take up my life where the old one finished, it is not possible. Maybe I will return to the lands of the high mountains, the quiet passes, the icy slopes. I long for the solitude of the thin air where I can meditate and still commune with my Father. I want to see the rainbows over the deafening waterfalls, feel the soft rain on my skin and endure the cleansing winds. There are still the despairing masses who I can give comfort and hope to.

There is one thing that I must do before all others, however. I am going to meet a man on the road to Damascus. At the moment his mind is filled with evil by Caiaphas. He is hell-bent on wiping out my converts, my friends and brothers. He is trying to obliterate all my words, my teachings and even the memory of me. I must change him to use all his energy and zeal in the opposite direction. He is blind but I will make him see again. I will even give him a new name as I did Peter. He will become, perhaps, the greatest of them all and carry my message to Rome itself.

I will give him a new covenant to replace that of Moses. His is but a pale shadow. It does not tell of the good things to come. I am the new covenant by sacrificing My blood for the sins of men. It will be through My laws, My teaching, My forgiveness that people will achieve the Kingdom of Heaven, through Me and Me alone. I am the way.

Because, Jofa, all your risks were taken for me and in my name, it will not be forgotten. You will be rewarded in heaven and remembered throughout eternity. Everything a man does should be in my name."

The flame flickered as the oil burned down low. Both men settled down to sleep after spending many hours talking, remembering, eating and drinking not a little wine. They were content to be together sharing their thoughts and memories as well as anticipating what might come in the future.

Joseph woke as the first rays of sunlight speared through the open porthole of the cabin. He was aware of the ship's movement. The oars were creaking and grinding to the muffled beat of the drum. Rubbing the sleep from his eyes, he cast round for Jeshua, so much loved and newly restored to him. He was the anointed one that God loved, the one who would inspire thousands, maybe millions in the years to come and he was here on this ship. Life was good. LochChaim!

Joseph went aloft to greet his friend. He searched the ship from stern to prow, port to starboard but found no sign of him anywhere on the ship. The coastline was fast disappearing below the horizon. Puzzled, he returned to his quarters muttering to himself,

"We ate, drank and talked together. Where can he be?"

There was only one silver goblet on the table with the remnants of unsupped wine. Had he dreamed the whole thing? Was it a vision sent by God? Had it all been real or just his imagination?

Joseph sighed. He was content in his mind that the Son of God was alive and well. He turned to his scrolls and charts to start the business of the day and his hand froze in space. His eyes noticed a mark on the table. He knew he had not been dreaming.

There in the dust was a crudely drawn, simple sketch of a fish.

Everything was very much all right with the world.